How To Conquer
# INIQUITY

## Satan's best kept secret.
## Man's biggest struggle.

### David L. Johnston

**Nothing But The Truth
Publications**

Unless otherwise indicated, Scripture quotations are taken from the King James Version (KJV) – public domain

Cover Design:
David Humphrey

Cover Photography:
Abby Lynn Humphrey

Cover Talent:
Joshua Humphrey

www.xulonpress.com

# Table of Contents

# Introduction

"Lord, what do you mean, *"I never knew you?"* The defendant stood before the Supreme Judge to give account of his life. "Everyone knows me! I was on international television! I had a deliverance ministry and I cast out demons *in your name!* Lord, there must be a mistake!"

Another soul, seeking to vindicate his position: "Lord, you commanded us to desire spiritual gifts and especially prophecy. I prophesied *in your name,* and people everywhere came to me for a prophetic word from You. Surely you know me!"

And yet another: "Lord, I built hospitals and orphanages and did many other wonderful works. And although my name is a household word among millions, Lord, I did all these things *in your name.* You must know me!"

The angel slowly perused the pages once more, but sadly shook his head. Again, the Holy Judge declared in a sorrowful tone, *"I never knew you. Depart from me ye workers of iniquity."*

As they were being led away from the presence of the Holy One of Israel, one looked back in wild-eyed confusion and cried out with a desperate plea, "Lord, how can casting out demons and prophesying and doing good works be *sin?"*

Strange, isn't it, how one can be a student of the Bible for his entire life and miss the obvious—the obvious truth that sin and iniquity are not the same.

In His just rejection, the Master did not say, "You sinners." He said, "You workers of iniquity."

Will someone please tell me, "What is iniquity?"

This book will answer that question.

# CHAPTER ONE

# My Secret Flaw

*"Then flew one of the seraphims unto me,*
*having a live coal in his hand,*
*which he had taken with the tongs*
*from off the altar:*

*And he laid it upon my mouth, and said,*
*Lo, this hath touched thy lips;*
*and thine iniquity is taken away,*
*and thy sin purged."*
(Isaiah 6:6-7)

Iniquity, Satan's best kept secret, is man's biggest struggle and it was my secret flaw. I was raised in a pastor's home and did not know the meaning of iniquity. I graduated from a Christian ministry preparatory college and still had learned nothing about iniquity. I entered the ministry not knowing I was full of iniquity and it was soon to destroy my life.

I appeared very successful. I spoke to the three thousand as graduation speaker. I was able to fill my itinerate preaching schedule well in advance. Little did I know that a 'time bomb' was secretly imbedded in my soul. I had a secret flaw.

I didn't sin much, even though I wanted to. Most of my sins happened in my mind, my imagination, and in disguise. I was taught that normal Christian life was defined by Paul in Romans seven: what I don't want to do, I do; and what I want to do, I don't do (Romans 7:19). What a miserable existence!

To make my predicament worse, my graduation class theme was based on the Isaiah six passage where the Lord asked, *"Who shall I send, and who will go for us?"* (Isaiah 6:8). Like Isaiah, we were all answering, *"Here am I; send me."* But the difference between Isaiah's preparation for the ministry and mine was as different as day and night.

An angel took a live coal off the altar and laid it upon Isaiah's mouth and declared, *"Thine iniquity is taken away, and thy sin purged."* Not me; I still had my iniquity—all of it!

I worked hard at the ministry. I tried to preach better, pray harder, lead further, sing sweeter, travel wider, say it funnier, play it cooler, insist more passionately, understand more completely, detail more fully, define more clearly, illustrate more dramatically, shock more effectively, and reach more numerically.

I read my Bible, memorized large portions of Scripture, and prayed earnestly. What others were doing in the ministry, I tried to do better.

I was a driven man. Can you imagine my shock when years later I discovered that I wasn't dedicated to the Lord at all, but to my iniquity? I wasn't working hard at the ministry. I was working hard at my iniquity.

It was secret. The Bible refers to iniquity as a mystery (2 Thessalonians 2:7). I had no idea of my flaw until I took on a special project. At a pastors' school I received a hand-out. On it, Bill Gothard challenged us to do a study on the difference between sin and iniquity. My iniquity made me believe that I was up for the challenge. Like everything else I did, I would do this with all of my heart. Actually, I did it with all the iniquity that was within me.

The discoveries were shocking! I almost quit the ministry. I found myself worthy of separation from God. I found myself so repulsive that I could say with Isaiah, *"Woe is me! for I am undone; because I am a man of unclean lips, and I dwell in the midst of a people of unclean lips: for mine eyes have seen the King, the LORD of hosts"* (Isaiah 6:5).

Because of the pressure of my iniquity, I decided to write my findings in a book and send it to all my preacher friends. Maybe such a book would make me famous. It was then that I realized that with all I knew about iniquity, I still had it. In spite of the encouragement of congregants to publish these truths, I could not. To write such a book would have added to my iniquity.

It's more than a decade later now. Although you may not understand it until you finish the read, it would now be iniquity not to write it. So here it is. I offer it to you in the spirit of repentance and shame— repentance, because I needed to change the structural motive of my life; shame, because my iniquity was so great.

This book is a journey of discovery: a discovery to uncover the truth about iniquity. You will learn that the anointed cherub set by God, who was upon the mountain of God, was perfect in his ways from the day that he was created, until iniquity was found in him (Ezekiel 28:14-15). You'll also discover the solutions. It is the primary reason Jesus came. *"Unto you first God, having raised up his Son Jesus, sent him to bless you, in turning away every one of you from his iniquities."* (Acts 3:26). Let's begin!

# CHAPTER TWO

## Sin and Iniquity
## Are Not the Same

*"But he was wounded
For our transgressions,
He was bruised
For our iniquities."*
(Isaiah 53:5)

Four distinct benefits of Calvary are described by Isaiah. In reference to the eternal work of Jesus on our behalf, it is noted:

1. He was wounded for our transgressions.
2. He was bruised for our iniquities.
3. The chastisement of our peace was upon Him.
4. With His stripes we are healed (Isaiah 53:5).

Most of us know what sin is: *". . . for sin is the transgression of the law. And ye know that he was manifested to take away our sin"* (1 John 3:4-5). It is plain that twenty-five percent of what Christ did on the cross for us, was to take away our sins. Isaiah 53:5 tells us: *"He was wounded for our transgressions."* His work, however, did not end there: *"He was bruised for our iniquities."* Wounds are one thing, but bruising is quite another. Bruising, can be a much deeper wound which causes internal bleeding.

The passage goes on to emphasize what Jesus did for our iniquities. The next verse repeats the issue: *"the LORD hath laid on him the iniquity of us all"* (Isaiah 53:6). How important it was to Jesus that provision, no matter how painful, be made for our iniquities. To God, this is no trite issue. Only five verses later He addresses it yet again: *"He shall see of the travail of his soul, and shall be satisfied: by his knowledge shall my righteous servant justify many; for he shall bear their **iniquities**"* (Isaiah 53:11).

If Jesus dealt with both sin and iniquity, then both sin and iniquity must be dealt with; we can count on it. And, if His dealing with iniquity was so excruciating, we best not take this issue lightly. Virtually every Bible writer knew the differences between sin and iniquity. The following are some plain examples:

**Moses knew the difference between sin and iniquity.**

> *"And Moses made haste, and bowed his head toward the earth, and worshipped.*
>
> *And he said, If now I have found grace in thy sight, O Lord, let my Lord, I pray thee, go among us; for it is a stiffnecked people; and pardon our **iniquity** and our sin, and take us for thine inheritance."*
> (Exodus 34:8-9)

The word *and* is a conjunction, used to connect grammatically co-ordinating words, phrases, or clauses; it means *along* or *together with*, *as well as*, *in addition to* (Dictionary.com). It does not create apposition but it rather distinguishes one from the other.

**Job and his friends knew the difference between sin and iniquity.**

> *"That thou enquirest after mine **iniquity**, and searchest after my sin?"*
> (Job 10:6)

> *"If I sin, then thou markest me,*
> *and thou wilt not acquit me from **mine iniquity**."*
> (Job 10:14)

## David knew the difference.

> *"And David fled from Naioth in Ramah,*
> *and came and said before Jonathan,*
> *What have I done? **what is mine iniquity?***
> ***and what is my sin** before thy father,*
> *that he seeketh my life?"*
> (1 Samuel 20:1)

In Psalm 51, David's psalm of repentance after his adulterous relationship with Bathsheba, his treacherous dealings with the military, and his killing of Uriah, he implores the Lord to help him recover from both his sin and his iniquity in those matters:

> *"Wash me throughly from mine **iniquity**,*
> *and cleanse me from my **sin**."*
> (Psalm 51:2)

Both David's iniquity and his sin required an adequate solution before he could ever regain "the joy of his salvation." He beseeched the Lord:

> *"Hide thy face from my **sins**,*
> *and blot out all mine **iniquities**."*
> (Psalm 51:9)

As we read this Psalm, we cannot help but be struck with the sincerity, the desperation, and the urgency of getting iniquity resolved.

## Isaiah knew the difference.

The prophet not only had personal knowledge of having his own iniquities dealt with, but knew and warned the people of the consequences of iniquity:

> *"Behold, the LORD'S hand is not shortened,*
> *that it cannot save; neither his ear heavy,*
> *that it cannot hear:*

> *But your **iniquities** have separated*
> *between you and your God,*
> *and your **sins** have hid his face from you,*
> *that he will not hear."*
> (Isaiah 59:1-2)

Only a few verses later Isaiah charges, ". . . *their thoughts are thoughts of **iniquity**"* (Isaiah 59:7). Are we beginning now to see the importance of dealing with iniquity?

**Jeremiah knew the difference.**

The enemies of the prophet Jeremiah plotted to murder him. Jeremiah knew that the problem was not just their intent to sin—to break the law by murdering—but that iniquity was involved as well. That is why he cried out to God:

> *"Yet, LORD, thou knowest all their counsel*
> *against me to slay me: forgive not their **iniquity**,*
> *neither blot out their **sin** from thy sight,*
> *but let them be overthrown before thee;*
> *deal thus with them in the time of thine anger."*
> (Jeremiah 18:23)

Notice the significant word *neither*, which clearly differentiates between sin and iniquity. We shall soon see that you can commit iniquity without sin, but you cannot sin without committing iniquity.

God hopes that His sending of judgment will position His people so that He can wisely deal with both their iniquity and their sins:

> *"It may be that the house of Judah*
> *will hear all the evil which I purpose to do unto them;*
> *that they may return every man from his evil way;*
> *that I may forgive their **iniquity and their sin**."*
> (Jeremiah 36:3)

The messengers of God knew quite well the differences, the effects, the consequences, and the causes of iniquity. Like other prophets, Jeremiah wept over the iniquity of the people:

> *"Your **iniquities** have turned away these things,*
> *and your **sins** have withholden*
> *good things from you."*
> (Jeremiah 5:25)

Jeremiah clearly predicted that the Messiah—the Holy One of Israel, the Lord God Almighty, the Lord of Hosts—would provide, not only the basis for forgiveness of iniquity and sin, but the power to overcome both iniquity and sin. Jeremiah said the procurement was coming! Notice the cause-and-effect relationship between iniquity and sin. And be sure to see the advance notice given in these Scriptures of the joy, the praise, the honor, the good, and the prosperity that comes from properly resolving iniquity:

> *"And I will cleanse them from all their **iniquity**,*
> *whereby they have sinned against me;*
> *and whereby they have transgressed against me.*
>
> *And it shall be to me a name of joy*
> *a praise and an honour*
> *before all the nations of the earth,*
> *which shall hear all the good that I do unto them:*
> *and they shall fear and tremble for all the goodness*
> *and for all the prosperity that I procure unto it."*
> (Jeremiah 33:8-9)

## Ezekiel knew the difference.

Ezekiel spoke of iniquity and the results thereof in forty-six different verses. He knew iniquity. He saw it in the people. He saw how God judged it. He said even the heathen would understand:

> *"And the heathen shall know that the house of Israel*
> *went into captivity for their **iniquity**."*
> (Ezekiel 39:23)

In later chapters we shall learn important details from Ezekiel. He surely knew the difference.

**Daniel knew the difference.**

He prophesied the precise moment when Jesus would come to deal with iniquity:

> *"Seventy weeks are determined upon thy people*
> *and upon thy holy city,*
> *to finish the transgression,*
> *and to make an end of* **sins***,*
> *and to make reconciliation for* **iniquity***,*
> *and to bring in everlasting righteousness,*
> *and to seal up the vision and prophecy,*
> *and to anoint the most Holy."*
> (Daniel 9:24)

**Nehemiah knew the difference.**

Nehemiah knew that the opposition was motivated by iniquity:

> *"And cover not their* **iniquity***,*
> *and let not their* **sin** *be blotted out from before thee:*
> *for they have provoked thee to anger*
> *before the builders.*
>
> *So built we the wall;*
> *and all the wall was joined together*
> *unto the half thereof:*
> *for the people had a mind to work."*
> (Nehemiah 4:5-6)

**Hosea knew the difference.**

So perceptive was he that he exposed the priesthood. The ministry was filled with iniquity. He described it this way:

> *"They eat up the* **sin** *of my people,*
> *and they set their heart on their* **iniquity***.*

*And there shall be, like people, like priest:*
*and I will punish them for their ways,*
*and reward them their doings."*
(Hosea 4:8-9)

## Peter knew the difference.

Peter preached the necessity of the resurrection of Jesus as the adequate cure for iniquity:

*"Unto you first God,*
*having raised up his Son Jesus,*
*sent him to bless you,*
*in turning away every one of you*
*from his **iniquities**."*
(Acts 3:26)

## Paul knew the difference.

The apostle Paul required deliverance from iniquity by every believer. There was to be no option. Every genuine follower was to deal with iniquity. It was to him a foundational issue—a seal, if you please—a confirmation of those that belonged to the Lord:

*"Nevertheless the foundation of God*
*standeth sure, having this seal,*
*The Lord knoweth them that are his.*
*And, Let every one that nameth the name of Christ*
*depart from **iniquity**."*
(2Timothy 2:19)

## Jesus knew the difference better than anyone.

Iniquity was why He came, why He died, why He rose, and why He lives in us today. I repeat this verse, because the text is so worthy and must not be forgotten:

*"Unto you first God,*
*having raised up his Son Jesus,*
*sent him to bless you,*
*in turning away every one of you*
*from his **iniquities**."*
(Acts 3:26)

Redemption from iniquity is a large part of what makes us peculiar. Paul concluded these remarks with the instruction that we are to speak this message, to exhort, and even to rebuke if necessary, to see that iniquity comes to an end. We are to deal with iniquity with all authority and not let anyone despise us for doing so:

*"Looking for that blessed hope,*
*and the glorious appearing of the great God*
*and our Saviour Jesus Christ;*

*Who gave himself for us*
*that he might redeem us from all **iniquity**,*
*and purify unto himself a peculiar people,*
*zealous of good works.*
*These things speak, and exhort,*
*and rebuke with all authority.*
*Let no man despise thee.*
(Titus 2:13-15)

## Iniquity Is Worse Than Sin.

All wrongs are not equal. In America, our laws are based upon British Common Law and specifically from the eighteenth century works of William Blackstone. Punishments are meted out in accordance with the severity of the crime committed. The more serious the crime, the more serious the penalty. The consequences for petty theft and grand theft are quite different. So if one penalty is greater than another penalty, then it stands to reason that the greater penalty was for the greater crime.

In this passage we discover that the penalty for iniquity is greater than the penalty for sin; not just for any sin, but for the sin of sodomy:

> *"For the punishment of the **iniquity***
> *of the daughter of my people*
> *is greater than the punishment of the **sin** of Sodom,*
> *that was overthrown as in a moment..."*
> (Lamentations 4:6)

The next question we must resolve is, "What exactly is iniquity, and how does it differ from sin?"

## CHAPTER THREE

# What Is Iniquity?

*"Ye say,*
*'The way of the Lord is not equal.'*
*Hear now, O house of Israel;*
*Is not my way equal?*
*Are not your ways unequal?*

*When a righteous man turneth away*
*from his righteousness,*
*and committeth iniquity,*
*and dieth in them;*
*for his iniquity that he hath done*
*shall he die."*
(Ezekiel 18:25-26)

It was plain to see that the writers of Scripture consistently differentiated between sin and iniquity. How iniquity differs from sin is the paramount question. We know what sin is: *"Whosoever committeth sin transgresseth also the law: for sin is the transgression of the law"* (1 John 3:4).

For example, the law says, *"Thou shalt not steal"* (Exodus 20:15). If I steal I have broken the law, and by doing so, I have sinned. It is easy to know when you have sinned. In fact, sins can be counted. They are measurable; but not iniquity. Iniquities cannot be counted. They are too numerous.

*"Is not thy wickedness great*
*and thine **iniquities** infinite?"*
( Job 22:5)

Iniquity is referred to as a mystery. Why? Because it is cloaked. Sin is a matter of black and white. When we sin we know it. But iniquity often wears disguises:

*" . . . For the mystery of **iniquity** doth already work . . ."*
(2 Thessalonians 2:7)

## How do we know what iniquity is?

Where can we get a clear definition or understanding? The answer lies in the following:

1. By the definition of the word
2. By the etymology
3. By the characteristics listed in Scripture
4. By the Biblical illustrations and examples
5. By the implications of a text
6. By the words in the original languages

## The Definition

The Webster 1828 dictionary describes iniquity as *a particular deviation from rectitude.* The Oxford English Dictionary (OED) describes iniquity as *want or violation of equity* [uneven, unequal].

Iniquity simply means *lacking equity or lacking equivalence.* It means *not equal to what it should be equal to.* The word is a legal term. If a punishment was not suited or equal to the crime it was called *an iniquity.*

In order to be sure of what the Bible means by the use of iniquity we should let the Bible itself illustrate the meaning of the word. This will make it very clear.

**Iniquity turned an archangel into Satan, the Devil.**

Let us go to the origin of iniquity, when it first showed up in the universe. Referring to Lucifer, who was once an archangel (a ruling class of angels) and an anointed cherub equal in status to Michael and Gabriel, this passage describes what happened. God never made the Devil. God made an archangel that became the Devil:

> *"Thou art the anointed cherub that covereth;*
> *thou hast walked up and down*
> *in the midst of the stones of fire.*
>
> ***Thou wast perfect*** *in thy ways*
> *from the day that thou wast created,*
> ***till iniquity was found in thee."***
> (Ezekiel 28:14-15) [See Appendix Six]

God says that He made and anointed this cherub and set him in his status. He (Lucifer) was on the holy mountain of God. He walked up and down in the midst of the stars (the stones of fire). Lucifer was not born; he was created by God. And Lucifer was perfect in his ways until iniquity was found in him.

Lucifer did not go out and sin. He became iniquitous. Certainly he sinned later, but what changed this archangel into the Devil was iniquity.

In order to help us with an accurate definition of iniquity, however, we must go to the passage that describes this turning of Lucifer into an iniquitous being. That description will define for us exactly what God means by iniquity. Remember, Lucifer was perfect until iniquity was found in him. Now here is the passage that describes how he became iniquitous:

> *"How art thou fallen from heaven,*
> *O Lucifer, son of the morning*
> *how art thou cut down to the ground,*
> *which didst weaken the nations!*

*For thou hast said in thine heart,*
*I will ascend into heaven,*
*I will exalt my throne above the stars of God:*
*I will sit also upon the mount of the congregation,*
*in the sides of the north*
*I will ascend above the heights of the clouds;*
*I will be like the most High."*
(Isaiah 14:12-14)

How did Lucifer fall? He "said in his heart." Here we learn that iniquity is first of all a heart condition; a heart condition that caused Lucifer to make five statements which indicate the heart condition of iniquity.

**Lucifer's Five Manifestations of Iniquity:**
1. I will ascend into heaven.
2. I will exalt my throne above the stars of God.
3. I will sit upon the mount of the congregation.
4. I will ascend above the heights of the clouds.
5. I will be like the most High.

Here iniquity is plainly defined. It is the condition of the heart that desires to be unequal with the will of God, to what He made us to be, or to what He wants us to do. It is selfishness. It is setting up the ego in the place—the rightful place—of God in our lives.

Lucifer was not content to be under God and equal with Gabriel and Michael. He wanted to be equal with God. He put his ideas on a par with God's ideas. He wanted to occupy God's position. He wanted to sit in the seat of authority and be in charge of the congregation. He wanted to be in the same position as God! In fact, he wanted to be above God.

This, my friend, was Lucifer's treason and it is our ultimate treason: attempting to take over the rulership position of God. It is the enthronement of self in the management place of God in our lives. This is iniquity. This is iniquity out of which flows iniquities and sins.

The Old Testament Hebrew word `avon (Strong's #5771) is translated 219 times out of 314 times in the King James Version as *iniquity* and literally means *perverse*. Perverse means *off track*, which means *not equal to the path*. This meaning is the same. It is only analogically different.

Forty-seven times the Hebrew word *'aven* (Strong's #0205) is used, almost always in the context of *workers of iniquity*—doing useless work other than what one should be doing (i.e., not equal to the right work or just work).

The word `evel (Strong's #5766) is used thirty-five times and is translated *evil*. Again the meaning is simply *to do what one should not be doing* (i.e., not equal to what one should be doing).

The New Testament Greek word *anomia* (Strong's #0458) is translated *iniquity* in the King James Version and literally means *illegality* or *not equal to the law*.

However, the clearest picture we have comes from the Scriptural accounts. The Bible is the best interpreter of itself. For our working definition we will use the following: Iniquity is the condition of the heart that desires to be unequal with our station in life, the will of God, what He made us to be, or what He wants us to do (as clearly expressed in His written Word). Iniquity: in-equity (in = not) (equity = equality) (in-equitable). Hence not equal, non-equivalent.

Now let us seek a practical understanding of this, first as it relates to Satan and then as it relates to us. Note that Lucifer wanted to change places with God. This intention of his heart constituted iniquity—not being equal to his station, to the will of God, to what he was designed to be, or to what he was made to do.

Lucifer, not accepting his proper station in the created order of things, attempted to change his rank from that of archangel to equality or superiority to God. This was his iniquity, and it is represented by the five statements Lucifer spoke in his heart—each beginning with "I will"—which we covered earlier.

What was the consequence of Lucifer's iniquity? The next verse tells us; *"Yet thou shalt be brought down to hell, to the sides of the pit"* (Isaiah 14:15).

At the precise moment of iniquity, Lucifer became the Devil—Satan—and was cast down. It's about the *how*. Remember how the passage began, *"How art thou fallen from heaven, O Lucifer, son of the morning! how art thou cut down to the ground. . . ."* (Isaiah 14:12).

The precise meaning of iniquity is not only illustrated in Scripture but is clearly stated in the following Ezekiel passage. This chapter is most often known for the verse, *". . . the soul that sinneth, it shall die"* (Ezekiel 18:4), however, this eighteenth chapter deals extensively with iniquity. In it, the people are accusing God of iniquity, but He affirms it is they that have the problem of iniquity. Note the interchangeability of the word *iniquity* with the *equal/unequal* issue.

*"Yet ye say, The way of the Lord is **not equal**.*
*Hear now, O house of Israel;*
*Is not my way equal? are not your ways **unequal**?*

*When a righteous man*
*turneth away from his righteousness,*
*and committeth **iniquity**, and dieth in them;*
*for his **iniquity** that he hath done shall he die."*
(Ezekiel 18:25-26)

You can tell from these verses that iniquity was not only the issue with Lucifer but is the problem of those who were purportedly the Lord's people, the house of Israel. The issue of iniquity is not a secondary issue. We will discover it to be the primary issue, the essence of wrong, the fundamental damning characteristic, and the cause of all sin, death, and the ruin of mankind. Note carefully these additional verses:

*"Yet saith the house of Israel,*
*The way of the Lord is **not equal**.*
*O house of Israel, are not my ways **equal**? are not your ways **unequal**?*

*Therefore I will judge you, O house of Israel,*
*every one according to his ways, saith the Lord GOD.*
*Repent, and turn yourselves*
*from all your transgressions;*
***so iniquity shall not be your ruin.***"
(Ezekiel 18:29-30)

Beloved Reader, be careful not to skim over these thoughts of God. Notice God's verdict: it is iniquity that causes the ruin of a man, a woman, a boy, a girl, a nation, a culture, the planet. It is mankind, and not God, that has iniquity.

## Iniquity causes narcissism.

Narcissism is the child of iniquity. *Narcissism* is *the egotistical admiration of one's self,* a concept introduced by Sigmund Freud into psychoanalytic theory. The term originated in Greek mythology where a young hunter, Narcissus, was so fixated with himself that he fell in love with the reflection of his own image in a pool of water (where he died).

The American Psychiatric Association has classified narcissism as a personality disorder in its *Diagnostic and Statistical Manual of Mental Disorders.* In my view the APA has severely underestimated the percentage of the population that have this "disorder." Identified traits of narcissism include, but are not limited to, the following:

Self-focus in any interpersonal relationship
Inability to sustain genuine relationships
Inability to empathize with others
Hypersensitivity to criticism or insults, real or imagined
Haughtiness
Disgust towards others who don't affirm them
Exploitation and manipulation of others for personal profit
Pretending self-importance
Exaggerating their importance, their achievements, their intentions

Thinking themselves as the ultimate authority and expert in everything
Inability to see life from any perspective but their own
Jealous and envious of others
Ungratefulness

Narcissism, in its varying degrees, has blatant disregard for the warning of Scripture:

*"For I say . . . to every man that is among you,*
*not to think of himself more highly*
*than he ought to think;*
*but to think soberly,*
*according as God hath dealt*
*to every man the measure of faith."*
(Romans 12:3)

Every one of us has been given a measured potential, a gifting if you please, of proper faith in ourselves. True joy in life comes from discovering our potential—our gift—and developing it and using it for the highest glory of God and others. Our measured potential is our identity. Iniquity causes us to be constantly comparing ourselves with others, competing and playing the one-up-manship game. And so we lose ourselves, our *real* selves. We're too busy trying to be something or somebody we're not. The tragedy is that there is no one left to be the real us. We've stolen our own identities. Hence the warning of Scripture:

*"For we dare not make ourselves of the number,*
*or compare ourselves with some*
*that commend themselves:*

*but they measuring themselves by themselves,*
*and comparing themselves among themselves,*
*are not wise.*

*But we will not boast of things without our measure,*
*but according to the measure of the rule*
*which God hath distributed to us,*
*a measure to reach even unto you.*
*For we stretch not ourselves beyond our measure . . ."*
(2 Corinthians 10:12-14)

What a tragedy, to have crossed the stage of time, be standing at the exit sign of life, and to look back and to have never discovered our true worth, our true selves, our purpose; iniquity coerced us into trying to be something we were never intended to be. Our real identities were never known. We were an imitation, our authenticity lost, never discovering the real, wonderful person—the person that God made—an original, not a copy, not a clone, but an indispensable, one of a kind *first edition.*

Conquering iniquity will free you to discover the real, wonderful you.

**Iniquity is a two-edged sword.**

Iniquity cuts two ways: up and down. It can make us narcissistic with exaggerated opinions (unequal) of ourselves on one side. But it also cuts downward turning us into psychopaths or sociopaths, exhibiting iniquity by self-destructive behaviors. This is thinking less of ourselves than we should. Instead of thinking we are above everyone else, or equal with others, we think we are below everyone else. It is simply another form of in-equality; iniquity. It is self-annihilation versus narcissism. Oh, the pain of this. Oh, the pain!

The abused child, criticized and accused; condemned, mocked and ridiculed; scorned and berated; wounded and fractured; humiliated and embarrassed; and sometimes deserted. The desertion rate of children by their fathers in America now stands at forty-two percent. At least forty-two percent of children are unfathered: they are unloved, unnourished, unnurtured, and uncherished! When a child is told that he is stupid, he *might* believe it. Told enough times, and in enough ways, he *will* believe it, because belief comes from what he repeatedly hears. Now there is no dignity; no self-respect; no self-esteem; no self-regard; no self-confidence; no self-worth; no self-importance; no self. This is iniquity.

What shall these victims of iniquity do? Shall they wile away their time watching television? Shall they spend their days trying to build up some synthetic self-image based on winning video games? What do children in this condition do? Will they turn to violence and vent their frustrated emptiness on others? I say the answer is to defeat the iniquity in their lives, to return to their real father, the Heavenly Father whose child they are—made in His likeness, created in His image, a son or daughter of the Most High. Let them forsake this iniquity of being less than God made them to be, forsake their thoughts of despair *". . . and let him return unto the Lord, and He will have mercy upon him; and to our God, for He will abundantly pardon"* (Isaiah 55:7). Let their languishing be turned to laughter. I hope you will say, "Amen!"

Our culture is polarized by these two forms of iniquity: those who think they are better than everyone else, and those who think everyone else is better than they. But it gets worse.

### Iniquity-Induced Schizophrenia and Bipolar Disorder.

Schizophrenia is classified as a mental disorder, an abnormal social behavior with the inability to recognize what is real. The symptoms can include unclear and confused thinking. It has a paralyzing effect on relationships. Schizophrenia comes from a Greek word, *skhizein* which means *to split*, and from *phren* which means *mind*. A split mind is confused. It vacillates from one form of thought to another, and often those thoughts are antithetical, juxtaposed and contradictory. **I am not a psychologist, so for clarification on terms it might be best to consult the professionals.**

However, many, many people are *split*. They fluctuate between the two extremes: from high to low; from elation to depression; from self-glory to self-deprecation; from narcissism to self-destructive behaviors, Thus there is no anchor, no sense of establishment, no reality. Personally, I think that MPS (Multiple Personality Disorder) is a wrong diagnosis. Bipolar, previously known as Manic Depression, may be an accurate description of the condition. One goes from extreme happiness to extreme irritability, from high energy to low energy, from elation to helplessness and hopelessness, from up times to down times. The mood swings are from extreme to extreme, from one pole to another pole (thus the term bipolar). These mood swings can happen in mere minutes, or over several days, or even over several weeks.

I am a Bible reader because I want to know the truth, and the Bible describes the above condition as being *"double minded."* First, let's look at the Scripture, then observe its application. In the context of asking for wisdom it says:

*". . . ask in faith, nothing wavering.*

*For he that wavereth is like a wave of the sea driven with the wind and tossed.*

*For let not that man think that he shall receive any thing of the Lord. A double minded man is unstable in all his ways."*
(James 1:6-8)

Let's observe:
  1) No wavering.
  2) Wavering is being tossed about like a wave of the sea.
  3) Wavering is being driven.
  4) Being driven means you are out of control.
  5) Not being in control is caused by a *"double mind."*
  6) Double-minded means double-thinking.
  7) A double-minded condition creates instability.
  8) The instability affects every area of one's life.

This is a Biblical diagnosis. The problem is double mindedness! But brace yourself now. Get ready for an ultimate understanding of this condition. This Scripture is about your personal identity, value, and worth. It is about resolving iniquity:

> *"Let the brother of low degree*
> *rejoice in that he is exalted:*
>
> *But the rich, in that he is made low:*
> *because as the flower of the grass*
> *he shall pass away."*
> (James 1:9-10)

The brother who thinks he is lower because he lacks money is brought up to equal. The rich man who thinks he's special and higher because of his money is brought down to equal. Mental health, emotional strength, and social stability are at stake here. The fix is in conquering iniquity.

## How Iniquity Applies To Us

In order to understand iniquity as our human predicament, we must first understand our place in the created order of things. The following is an important summary statement.

In terms of our station in life we are created to be:
> Under God
> Equal With Others
> Over Satan

It should also be noted that we are to be under rightful authorities who are operating within the jurisdiction of that authority. All rightful authority has definition, parameters, limitations. Most errors about authority are derived from one of two sources; 1) ascribing more authority to someone than the position warrants; 2) ascribing less authority to someone other than the position warrants. All human authority has limits and qualifications assigned to it. Those limits are defined by Scripture. For example, a husband has a certain authority over his wife but only if he meets the qualification of loving her as Christ loved the church and gave himself for it (Ephesians 5:25). God is the ONLY absolute authority.

Thus our station in life can also be defined as:
> Under God
> Under Rightful Authorities
> Equal with Others
> Over Satan

# Chapter Four

# The Spiritual Implications of Iniquity

*"How much more*
*abominable and filthy is man,*
*which drinketh iniquity like water?"*
(Job 15:16)

**1. Iniquity is hated by God.**

Oh Beloved, Oh that we would love what God loves and hate what God hates. We now get an insight into God's heart; yes, into His thoughts and, if you can imagine it, we can feel His feelings. Like me, you have probably had profound and almost out-of-body experiences like the Apostle Paul, contemplating the great things of God. We stand in awe of Him. We behold the beauty of the Lord, the majesty and the grandeur of His great person. Who is likened unto Him? But knowing God intimately has another side to it. It was described by the Apostle Paul in his great proclamation, *"That I might know Him . . . in the fellowship of His suffering"* (Philippians 3:10). We know and experience the pains of God as well. May I draw the curtain back from the heart of God for a moment? Will you be tender, sensitive, and respectful? I shudder sometimes to say what I am about to say; to tell what I'm about to tell. To put this in writing is, for me, quite traumatic. Go with me sacredly. Walk very softly with me. We tread on holy ground here.

Three words, three obscure words spoken by God changed me forever. These three words are really God exposing His heart of hearts. These words are spoken in the midst of a righteous outpouring of wrath. They are a shocking revelation. They don't last long, only three words. The curtain quickly closes again. It's just a glimpse. Here they are: *"I am broken"* (Ezekiel 6:9).

God broken? Please, please tell me this cannot be true! He uses twenty more words to tell us why: *". . . with their whorish heart, which hath departed from me, and with their eyes, which go a whoring after their idols . . ."* (Ezekiel 6:9). We have eyes—adulterous eyes—whorishly rejecting Him to pursue those things which are no gods at all. But we have made them so. And our eyes betray the whorishness of our hearts. So, Dear Reader, this is what it is like to *"know Him in the fellowship of His sufferings"* (Philippians 3:10).

Hurt is proportional to love. This is the first instruction on love from the famous thirteenth chapter of 1 Corinthians: *"Love suffers long."*

*Love suffers long and is kind* (back to the one who is the cause of the suffering). When you love someone, their hurt becomes your hurt. The very idea of someone beating one of my daughters or one of my grandchildren is painful enough. I would rather have my poor body afflicted than theirs. Loving God means hurting over the things that hurt Him. And what is that? The rejection, the treason, the trade-off of allegiance from God to that which is a phony, a non God—me! King me! Oh, the depth of iniquity when men play god. Playing god requires the usurpation of the real God, getting rid of his authority over us so we can rule unchallenged.

Samuel experienced this fellowship with God, when upon the mountain God said, *". . . they have not rejected thee, but they have rejected me, that I should not reign over them"* (1 Samuel 8:7).

The most blatant anti-God condition of any being in the universe is that of being iniquitous. It deserves to be hated by God and man. We play God. We usurp. We deny Him His Lordship. We say, "We will not have Him rule over us." We will decide what's right and wrong. We exalt our puny ideas against the high and holy thoughts of God. Oh God, deliver us from our iniquity! We want fellowship with Thee:

*"The foolish shall not stand in thy sight:*
*thou hatest all* **workers of iniquity.** *"*
(Psalm 5:5)

*Shall the* **throne of iniquity** *have fellowship with thee,*
*which frameth mischief by a law?*
(Psalm 94:20)

*For thus saith the high and lofty One*
*that inhabiteth eternity, whose name is Holy;*
*I dwell in the high and holy place,*
*with him also that is of a contrite and humble spirit,*
*to revive the spirit of the humble,*
*and to revive the heart of the contrite ones.*

*For* **the iniquity of his covetousness** *was I wroth . . ."*
(Isaiah 57:15, 17)

Iniquity fails to see any difference in status between itself and God. Beloved, the gap between us, the created, and Him, the Creator, is immense. He is high and lifted up. He is holy. I love the quote by A.W.Tozer:

God is above all things and beneath all things.
God is outside all things and inside all things.
God is above but not pushed up.
God is beneath but not pressed down.
God is outside but not excluded.
God is inside but not confined.
God is above all things presiding
Beneath all things sustaining.
God is outside all things embracing
Inside all things filling.

Iniquity is hated by Christ. We know many thing by the straight-forward statements of Scripture. They are sentences that require no guessing as to their meaning or interpretations, and they contain no ambiguities. The plain statement of Scripture regarding the disposition of Jesus on the matter of iniquity is such a declaration. Here it is:

*"Thou hast loved righteousness, and* **hated iniquity;** *"*
(Hebrews 1:9)

## 2. God has no iniquity at all.

I love ten thousand things about God. Someday I'd like to list them—all of them. I'd probably never get to the end of the list, because He is infinite, and I will be forever discovering more of His greatness. But here is one of the ten thousand plus things I like and love about God: He has, and does, no iniquity—zero! How great is this? It is one (and only one) of His infinite attributes of greatness. Take a look:

*"Give ear, O ye heavens, and I will speak;*
*and hear, O earth, the words of my mouth.*

*My doctrine shall drop as the rain,*
*my speech shall distil as the dew,*
*as the small rain upon the tender herb,*
*and as the showers upon the grass:*

*Because I will publish the name of the LORD:*
*ascribe ye greatness unto our God.*
*He is the Rock, his work is perfect:*
*for all his ways are judgment:*

*a* ***God of truth and without iniquity,***
*just and right is he."*
(Deuteronomy 32:1-4)

## 3. Iniquity is the enemy of God.

The universe is a moral universe, meaning that the universe is occupied by moral beings: beings who can choose right or wrong, peace or anarchy. Sustainability is dependent on some structure, some ascribed hierarchy, and specific roles with defined latitude or parameters. Peaceful and constructive co-existence cannot existentially endure if *"everyone does what's right in his own eyes,"* if everyone plays God. Iniquity is playing God, being and doing what Satan attempted: not only to be equal with God, but setting himself above God. *"I will exalt my throne above the stars of God:"* (Isaiah 14:13)

Now God is not insecure in this power struggle. He has all the power. Perhaps God is not so much concerned about power, as He is about love and wisdom. He is attempting to populate the universe with beings who love, who choose the highest good of the universe and others without personal benefit as the driving force. Iniquity is the antithesis of His philosophy, His love-philosophy! And so it is right, wise, and loving for Him to oppose such a damaging anarchistic-producing viewpoint summed up by the word, iniquity. The Holy God understands the evil thereof. He opposes iniquity not because of some self-aggrandizing scheme to make Himself the top honcho, but because He is the only one wise and loving enough to hold the position of God:

> *"Art thou not from everlasting,*
> *O LORD my God, mine Holy One?*
> *Thou art of purer eyes than to behold evil,*
> *and canst not look on **iniquity** . . ."*
> (Habakkuk 1:12-13)

## 4. Iniquity is hated by Christ.

We know many thing by the straight forward statements of Scripture. They are sentences that require no guessing as to their meaning, no ambiguities, and no interpretations necessary. The plain statement of Scripture regarding the disposition of Jesus on the matter of iniquity is such a declaration. Here it is:

*"Thou hast loved righteousness, and hated iniquity;"*
(Hebrews 1:9)

## 5. Iniquity is characteristic of being anti-Christ.

*Against Christ.* What a horrible indictment. The Anti-Christ—a person who is against Christ— opposes God, puts himself above all the things of God, and establishes himself as the man in charge. The identity of this person is still a mystery, not yet revealed. But everything he is and does is categorized as iniquity.

Do you know people who put their opinions above the opinions of God; who exalt their ideas above the written Words of God; who refuse God's management of their lives; who pride themselves as self-made; who are willful and assertive, as opposed to yielded and zealous for the will of God? Iniquity is the spirit of antichrist, right now at work in the world (and in the church). The mystery of iniquity is already working:

*"Let no man deceive you by any means:*
*for that day shall not come,*
*except there come a falling away first,*
*and that man of sin be revealed, the son of perdition;*

*Who opposeth and exalteth himself*
*above all that is called God,*
*or that is worshipped;*
*so that he as God sitteth in the temple of God,*
*shewing himself that he is God.*

*. . . For **the mystery of iniquity** doth already work . . ."*
(2 Thessalonians 2:3-7)

## 6. Iniquity is often religious.

One would hope that Christianity and the church would be a place of refuge from all that is in the world: a sanctuary, a safe place free from contamination that surrounds us in the work place. But, such is not the case.

Ezekiel was told by the Lord to dig a tunnel, so he dug to a hole in the wall of the house of God. God said, *"Go in and behold the wicked abominations that they do there"* (Ezekiel 8:7-9). What he saw was the great wickedness in the imaginations of the priests.

Eventually, he got to the inner courts of the Lord's house (v.16) and he saw that false worship was taking place. The passage goes on to confirm that the hidden iniquities and wickedness of the spiritual leaders had a profound effect on the land. As the church goes, so goes the world. When the salt has lost its savor, *". . . it is thenceforth good for nothing, but to be cast out, and to be trodden under foot of men"* (Matthew 5:13). When the light of God is extinguished from the church, darkness will cover the land. The church is no longer functioning as God intended.

*"Ah sinful nation, a people laden with **iniquity,***
*a seed of evildoers,*
*children that are corrupters:*
*they have forsaken the LORD,*
*they have provoked the Holy One of Israel unto anger,*
*they are gone away backward.*

*Why should ye be stricken any more?*
*ye will revolt more and more:*
*the whole head is sick, and the whole heart faint.*

*From the sole of the foot even unto the head*
*there is no soundness in it;*

*but wounds, and bruises, and putrifying sores:*
*they have not been closed, neither bound up,*
*neither mollified with ointment."*
*(Isaiah 1:4-6)*

Israel was meant to be a nation different from all nations, separated unto God; but they backslid, and the backsliding showed up as iniquity, as well as sinfulness. This text shows what iniquity does to a once righteous people:

1. Breeds evildoing
2. Begets children who are corrupters
3. Causes them to forsake the Lord
4. Provokes God to anger
5. Causes them to go backward
6. Causes them to revolt
7. Causes mental disorders
8. Causes heartlessness
9. Causes sickness

Israel still carried on the forms of Godliness in their religious observances and customs, but iniquity took away the substance of Godliness; so much so that God called their religious practices an abomination. Iniquity reached into their prayer meetings, their holy days, their Sabbaths, their worship, and even their fasting:

*"Bring no more vain oblations;*
*incense is an abomination unto me;*
*the new moons and sabbaths,*
*the calling of assemblies, I cannot away with;*
**it is iniquity,** *even the solemn meeting."*
(Isaiah 1:13)

Jesus Himself made it very clear that people, including ministers, could be doing many activities which appeared to be very spiritual, but were in fact the fruit and offspring of iniquity. This included prophesying in His name, casting out devils in His name, and doing many wonderful works:

*"Many will say to me in that day,*
*Lord, Lord, have we not prophesied in thy name?*
*and in thy name have cast out devils?*
*and in thy name done many wonderful works?*

*And then will I profess unto them, I never knew you:*
*depart from me, **ye that work iniquity.**"*
(Matthew 7:22-23)

Ministers can be motivated not by God, to do what they should be doing, but by iniquity. Competition and rivalry between ministries, the desire to be bigger and better than other ministries, is rooted in iniquity, albeit, these motives are usually kept secret. After all, we wouldn't want others to see the real wickedness of our hearts. I didn't.

## 7. Iniquity is the cause of all sin.

The first sin in the Bible was preceded by the first iniquity in the Bible. The act of disobedience was motivated by the iniquity of *"ye shall be as gods."*(Genesis 3:5)

We can do iniquity without sin, but we cannot sin without iniquity. In the following text we must pay close attention to the word, whereby. Whereby means by which, through which, by means of which, because of which. You can discern the causative nature of the term. In this Scripture we learn the cause and effect relationship of iniquity and transgression. Notice the term "whereby," is used three times:

*"And I will cleanse them from all **their iniquity,***
***whereby they have sinned** against me;*
*and I will pardon all their **iniquities,***
***whereby they have sinned,***
***and whereby** they have transgressed against me.*

*And it shall be to me a name of joy,*
*a praise and an honour*
*before all the nations of the earth . . ."*
(Jeremiah 33:8-9)

And just what do we need? Cleansing! Pardon! And that's exactly where we are heading.

## 8. Iniquity caused seven effects in Sodom.

There is a vast difference between the sins of Sodom and the iniquities of Sodom. The Scriptures record both. Notice that most of these are not sins at all, but they are iniquities and wicked, none-the-less. Here, we let the Scriptures speak for themselves:

*"Behold, **this was the iniquity** of thy sister Sodom*
*pride, fulness of bread, and abundance of idleness*
*was in her and in her daughters,*
*neither did she strengthen the hand of the poor and needy.*

*And they were haughty, and committed*
*abomination before me:*
*therefore I took them away as I saw good."*
(Ezekiel 16:49-50)

Was Sodom destroyed for her sins? Most assuredly. But Sodom was also destroyed for her iniquities. This Scripture lists them:

Pride, self-exaltation
Over-consumption
Misuse of time
Slothfulness in children
Insensitivity to the poor
Arrogance
Abomination

## 9. Iniquity prevents effective prayer.

The basis of real prayer is contact with God. Prayer is not astral-projection. Prayer is not floating ideas off into the ethereal. Prayer is not psychological manipulation. And prayer is not twisting God's arm to get Him to do what He already says He will do. Prayer is contact with God. Prayer is a dialogue, not a monologue. This implies He can hear us and we can hear Him: contact! It's real! Vital! Meaningful!

Many have given up on prayer, because they claim it doesn't work. They are merely frustrated, because they cannot get God to do their will; that's one reason many don't pray. After all, prayer is not about getting my will done on earth through heaven, but more about getting His will done on earth through me.

Iniquity poses two prayer problems: First, we cannot get God, with all His wisdom and resources, to become the servant of our iniquity. He is against iniquity altogether, so the agenda of iniquity, no matter how beautifully or artfully communicated, will not stir God's interest at all—zero! Secondly, He doesn't even hear, let alone answer.

*"If I regard iniquity in my heart,*
*the Lord will not hear me."*
(Psalm 66:18)

Does God still answer prayer? Most assuredly. He is as powerful as ever. And He is as motivated as ever to participate with you and me. But herein lies the problem:

*"Behold, the LORD'S hand is not shortened,*
*that it cannot save;*
*neither his ear heavy, that it cannot hear:*

***But your iniquities** have separated*
*between you and your God,*
*and your sins have hid his face from you,*
*that he will not hear."*
(Isaiah 59:1-2)

Iniquity tries to get God, with all His power and with all His wisdom, to do what we want. Iniquity is an assertion of self-will. In prayer, iniquity attempts to induce God to participate. But He will not.

## 10. Iniquity prevents us from kneeling or bowing down.

Like the hypocrites referred to by Jesus, we don't mind standing to pray. But kneeling is not all that popular, except in some traditional, symbolic, and liturgical ways. I've sung songs about kneeling without kneeling. I could sing lies so easily. Yet isn't it true, that nothing could be more beautiful than for the created to bow before the Creator? Oh God, Thou Magnificent, I yield to you. Let my heart ever be soft.

*"O come, let us worship and bow down:*
*let us kneel before the LORD our maker.*

*For he is our God;*
*and we are the people of his pasture,*
*and the sheep of his hand.*
*To day if ye will hear his voice,*
*Harden not your heart . . ."*
(Psalm 95:6-7)

## 11. Iniquity causes the loss of love for God and others.

Iniquity destroys love, because it is a heart condition entirely op-posed to genuine love. Iniquity has its own selfish agenda, so it will create the appearance of love (because it is good PR to seem so). Iniquity knows how to show love without actually loving:

*"And many false prophets shall rise,*
*and shall deceive many.*
*And **because iniquity** shall abound,*
*the love of many shall wax cold."*
(Matthew 24:11-12)

# CHAPTER FIVE

# The Personal Effects of Iniquity

*"Let every one that nameth the name of Christ
depart from Iniquity."*
(2 Timothy 2:19)

### 1. Iniquity is personally destructive.

*You can't run a good race on the wrong track.* Iniquity is a wrong
track. The selfishness of iniquity can never be satisfied. The track
is a mine field. Pitfalls and disappointments abound. Consequences
interfere with significance and fulfillment. The Biblical description
is *"afflicted:"*

> *"Fools because of their transgression,
> and **because of their iniquities**, are afflicted."*
> (Psalm 107:17)

Iniquity cannot see straight. It is biased, yea perverted, in its out-
look. For example, an iniquity is touching the breasts of a stranger
(someone other than your wife). It seems attractive enough, in fact,
compelling. But look at the destructive consequences: snared and
bound, without instruction, full of folly, and off the track.

*"And why wilt thou, my son,*
*be ravished with a strange woman,*
*and embrace the bosom of a stranger?*

*His own iniquities shall take the wicked himself,*
*and he shall be holden with the cords of his sins.*

*He shall die without instruction; and in the*
*greatness of his folly he shall go astray."*
(Proverbs 5:20, 22-23)

## 2. Iniquity drains strength.

David the Psalmist, dealt with iniquity most of his life. This is what he said: *"my strength faileth because of mine **iniquity**"* (Psalm 31:10). This is true because iniquity causes us to spend excessive energy going in the wrong direction. As a result we waste time, and miss the genuine purpose God has for our lives.

## 3. Iniquity lifts up self, puts down others.

Iniquity makes us flatter ourselves. It gags me to realize how disgusting I've been in my day. Notice here (and we will see it again later) that iniquity shows in our speech. Wisdom disappears. We dream up big ideas for ourselves. We boast and fail to stand on principle against evil, being politically correct for our own self-advantage:

*"For he flattereth himself in his own eyes,*
*until his iniquity be found to be hateful.*

*The words of his mouth are iniquity and deceit*
*he hath left off to be wise, and to do good.*
*He deviseth mischief upon his bed;*
*he setteth himself in a way that is not good;*
*he abhorreth not evil."*
(Psalm 36:2-4)

*"How long shall they utter and speak hard things?*
*and all the workers of iniquity boast themselves?*

*They break in pieces thy people,*
*O LORD, and afflict thine heritage. "*
(Psalm 94:4-5)

## 4. Iniquity makes a good person bad.

In American politics we are often faced with a dilemma: a political party that blatantly endorses wrong. They make no bones about it. They are in favor of sexual perversion, killing babies, open borders,

non-enforcement of laws, etc. Then there's a party that looks good on the outside, says the right things, and comments favorably on moral principles, but is just as inept at enforcing laws, willing to cater to special interest groups, and just as subject to bribes. I'm not sure which is worse—one who looks like the enemy and is, or one that looks moral, but isn't.

Iniquity changes the motive and sometimes does the right things, but for the wrong resons. The young man that shows good manners when he comes to take your daughter out for a few hours, may open and close the door for her, bring flowers, and talk respectfully to you, her parents. But if you could see inside his heart, that his motive is to win your daughter's affections and your confidence—with the intent that he will eventually get to use her to please himself—you would change your mind. Those good manners become a cover-up for the real intentions of his heart. Now they become disgusting.

The motive, the ultimate intention behind everything we do, is fundamentally important. *"Man looketh on the outward appearance, but the Lord looketh on the heart"* (1 Samuel 16:7).

Iniquity is what makes righteousness filthy. This is the plain meaning of this oft misapplied Scripture:

*"But we are all as an unclean thing,*
*and all our righteousnesses are as filthy rags;*
*and we all do fade as a leaf;*
*and our **iniquities, like the wind, have taken us away.***"
(Isaiah 64:6)

Your righteousness is important to God. In fact, we learn that we are going to be clothed in righteousness when we, the Bride, meet Jesus, the Groom. That righteousness is the deeds of the saints:

*"Let us be glad and rejoice, and give honour to him:*
*for the marriage of the Lamb is come,*
*and his wife hath made herself ready.*

*And to her was granted that she should be arrayed*
*in fine linen, clean and white*
*for the fine linen is the righteousness of saints."*
(Revelations 19:7-8)

Iniquity changes it. Remember what it did to Lucifer. Iniquity is doing right things for wrong reasons:

*"Thou wast perfect in thy ways*
*from the day that thou wast created*
*till **iniquity** was found in thee."*
(Ezekiel 28:15)

## 5. Iniquity increases unto more iniquity.

Iniquity is hard to stop, hard to quit. That is, unless we know how, which is hopefully why you are reading this book. Be assured, God has adequate solutions and we will get to them. In the meantime, it should be noted that iniquity is like the proverbial snowball rolling downhill. It gathers momentum, rolling freely. The longer we wait to deal with iniquity, the more difficult. Fathers ought to train children at young ages to be iniquity-free.

*". . . for as ye have yielded your members*
*servants to uncleanness*
*and to **iniquity unto iniquity;***
*even so now yield your members servants*
*to righteousness unto holiness."*
(Romans 6:19)

## 6. Iniquity is contagious.

The tragedy of Sodom and Gomorrah is not really the tragedy of Sodom and Gomorrah. It is the tragedy of Lot, a man who had no influence for God. The city would have been saved had the angel been able to find a mere ten righteous persons. Most think Sodom was destroyed because of its sin, and in particular, the sin named after the city: sodomy. However, as we will learn, iniquity is behind the sin. Sodom was full of iniquity, and that it why it was judged:

*"And when the morning arose,*
*then the angels hastened Lot, saying,*
*Arise, take thy wife, and thy two daughters,*
*which are here; lest thou be consumed*
*in **the iniquity of the city.***"
(Genesis 19:15)

I've seen Sodom. From the top of Masada you can see the remains; the ashes outline the streets to this day. Most people can name the sins of Sodom but few can name its iniquities. The seven iniquities of Sodom are listed in Ezekiel 16:49. They're coming up in a moment.

## 7. Iniquity causes covetousness.

I've known about shopping. I've wanted the best, and if you can imagine, stuff I didn't even need. "I owe it to myself," had been my mantra. And so we grab and clutch and grasp endlessly, from one purchase to another to another to another; we are driven!

*"For the iniquity of his covetousness was I wroth . . ."*
(Isaiah 57:17)

## 8. Iniquity produces vanity.

*"He that soweth **iniquity** shall reap vanity:*
*and the rod of his anger shall fail."*
(Proverbs 22:8)

This verse is essentially saying that if our talents, our time and our treasure are motivated by iniquity, the results equal a big fat zero. Vanity means nothingness. What a tragedy to live life and when final calculations are made of the profit, the balance sheet shows zero. Life was just an empty box.

Vanity simply means lack of value, lack of significance, lack of worth. It seems that our culture loves the meaningless passage of time. Thus the Scriptures enquire, *"O ye sons of men... how long will ye love vanity?"* (Psalm 4:2)

*"Surely men of low degree are vanity,*
*and men of high degree are a lie:*
*to be laid in the balance,*
*they are altogether lighter than vanity."*
(Psalm 62:9)

Solomon, deemed the wisest man in history and a trillionaire, made an evaluation of *"everything under the sun."* His conclusion? *"vanity of vanities; all is vanity"* (Ecclesiastes 1:2). His investigation was thorough.

*"I have seen all the works that are done under the sun;*
*and, behold, all is vanity and vexation of spirit."*
(Ecclesiastes 1:14)

Solomon takes us through a litany of efforts to achieve happiness and meaning in life. . . to discover what really counts for time and eternity? Here is a short list of the things he evaluated:

| | |
|---|---|
| pleasure | houses |
| laughter | farm lands |
| wine | gardens |
| great buildings | orchards |

He concluded that all was, *"vanity and vexation of spirit."* I've asked myself many times why this "testimony" is in the Bible. I've concluded that God wants us, you and I, to learn from Solomon's experience so that we don't have to waste years of our life before coming to the same conclusion. By then we may be standing at the "exit" sign with nothing to show for it.

What's the cause of vanity? The answer is iniquity.
*"Woe unto them that draw iniquity with cords of vanity,*
*and sin as it were with a cart rope:*
*That say, Let him make speed,*
*and hasten his work, that we may see it:*
(Isaiah 5:18-19)

## 9. Iniquity prevents fellowship.

Iniquity carries with it a sense of superiority. It may be a concealed smugness, a self-satisfied, self-congratulatory, conceited belief in oneself. This inflated view of oneself tends to interfere with relationships, unless the other parties have bought into the superiority, or bow in obeisance.

*"The Pharisee stood and prayed thus with himself,*
*God, I thank thee, that I am not as other men are . . .*
*extortioners, unjust, adulterers, or even as this publican.*

*I fast twice in the week, I give tithes of all that I possess."*
(Luke 18:11-12)

"I am better than others," is the mantra, the sacred utterance of iniquity, albeit, not often spoken out loud to others but certainly acted out in relationships. Iniquity knows no peers, it only pretends them or is selective, choosing associations with those deemed to be higher up. Let us remember that we are designed to be under God, equal with others, and over Satan. There should be no divisions, especially in the church.

*"That there should be no schism in the body;*
*but that the members should have the same care*
*one for another."*
(1 Corinthians 12:25)

Notice the *"same care"* phrase. We are back to the issue of equality. The question is, how do we achieve fellowship. The answer is by having right attitudes toward one another: *"Let nothing be done through strife or vainglory; but in lowliness of mind let each esteem other better than themselves."* (Philippians 2:3)

Fellowship with one another is horizontal. Only fellowship with God is vertical. Fellowship with one another requires mutual acceptance and esteem. This lateral relationship is broken by iniquity, when one thinks of himself or herself as better than another.

## 10. Iniquity creates the illusion of prosperity.

You are an intended set of specifications, determined by God. This includes, but is not limited to, your time in history, your gender, your parentage, your mental potential, your giftings, and much more. If we don't discover these—and accept, appreciate, celebrate, and develop them—we become synthetic, substituting our own pursuits in the place of our intended reality. This unequalness to our real essence sends us off on a wild goose chase, so to speak. We learn how to pull our own strings, get the upper hand, and outdo the competition. Genuine self-acceptance gets lost amid the torrents of striving and rivalry.

But strive we do; and with discipline, determination, and consistency we can achieve what appears to be success. We have found shortcuts; we have cut corners; we have manipulated our way, and *voila* we have arrived (we think).

Appearances become all-important. Deception is born of this. Tricks, techniques, and maneuvers become a way of thinking, acting, and being. Authenticity gets lost in all of this. Self-aggrandizement, is done subtly, because we don't want anyone to think we are really doing what we're doing—enhancing and exaggerating our own importance. We ennoble everything we do. People buy into it. We are taught to "fake it 'til you make it." We run our own PR departments. *"Most men will proclaim every one his own goodness: but a faithful man who can find?"* (Proverbs 20:6).

However, God is not fooled. He says they only appear to flourish.

Aesop, the ancient creator of Aesop's Fables, knew that "appearances are often deceiving." Hollywood has lied to us. They have taught us that appearances are everything. Now we have style without substance.

Success can appear as financial prosperity, vocational achievement, social acceptance, or public applause (at least in one's own mind). The imaginary view of one's self is so empty compared with the relaxed, confident, tranquil, poised, mental, and emotional posture of reality:

> *"When the wicked spring as the grass,*
> *and **when all the workers of iniquity do flourish;***
> *it is that they shall be destroyed for ever:*
> *But thou, LORD, art most high for evermore.*
> *For, lo, thine enemies, O LORD,*
> *for, lo, thine enemies shall perish;*
> ***all the workers of iniquity shall be scattered."***
> (Psalm 92:7-9)

## 11. Iniquity is the cause of failures.

Many individuals go to pastors and counsellors in search of help. And well they should, for according to Psalm 20:2, "help is to be in the sanctuary." Those who know God and His ways should have it all figured out. It's not rocket science. The solution to every human ailment is in the Scriptures, and men and women of God know those solutions.

The problem, however, is compounded because those seeking help will often enquire about solutions to every problem except their real underlying issue. They will talk about respectable problems, but beneath those problems there is usually at least one unrespectable problem.

It is true that some people do not mind speaking of unrespectable problems. After all, doing so has been popularized by many of the afternoon quasi-help television programs, where they not only air their dirty laundry but forget the laundry and just air the dirt. Very gross. Very disgusting.

This is why a Christian counselor must function at a deeper level. By the way, what is a Christian counselor? Is it a Christian who counsels on the basis of Freud, Mowrer, Watson, Maslow, Jung, or Skinner? Or is a Christian counselor one who is in fact a Bible-based counsellor? You decide. The true Christian counselor must tap into another dimension, a spiritual dimension; because every person is a spirit, lives in a body, and possesses mind and emotion. God has provided us with help to do just that. Here's how:

*"And the spirit of the LORD shall rest upon him,*
*the spirit of wisdom and understanding,*
*the spirit of counsel and might,*
*the spirit of knowledge and of the fear of the LORD;*
*And shall make him of quick understanding*
*in the fear of the LORD:*
*and he shall not judge after the sight of his eyes,*
*neither reprove after the hearing of his ears:*
*But with righteousness shall he judge the poor,*
*and reprove with equity . . ."*
(Isaiah 11:2-4)

This foretelling is about Jesus, of course. However, it is also true of every conscientious Bible counselor. According to this Scripture, here is what a Bible counselor needs:

1) The spirit of the Lord
2) The spirit of wisdom
3) The spirit of understanding
4) The spirit of counsel
5) The spirit of might
6) The spirit of knowledge
7) The spirit of the fear of the Lord

These are referred to as the "Seven Spirits of God," in Revelation 3:1. It gets much better, because this counselor gets enormous benefits as listed in this same Scripture.

1) Quick understanding
2) The ability to adjudicate from what cannot be seen with the eye
3) The ability to correct, not based on what's been told to the hearing of the ear
4) The ability to judge matters rightly, correctly
5) The ability to *"reprove with equity,"* to counteract the imbedded iniquity in matters.

Now we come to the crux of counseling issues. Beyond trying to fix symptoms, deeper than the cause-and-effect levels of behaviorism, we reach to the root of every matter. The Bible calls it, "the stumbling block of iniquity":

> *"And the word of the LORD came unto me, saying,*
> *Son of man,*
> *these men have set up their idols in their heart,*
> *and put **the stumblingblock of their iniquity***
> *before their face:*
> *should I be enquired of at all by them?*
> (Ezekiel 14:2-3)

This is the root of all behavioral matters. Their iniquity is their stumbling block. Then God asks a rhetorical question, *"should I be enquired of at all by them?"* Why should they ask God for help when the root is iniquity-caused idolatries? They want help for their surface-problems, but that is not the root of their problem.

A stumbling block is an impediment, a hindrance, a handicap, an obstacle, a bar, a fetter, a hurdle, a shackle, an encumbrance, or a snare. A stumbling block is something that trips you up, that causes a fall. The stumbling block of iniquity is the greatest cause of failure.

The solutions for human predicaments are generally quite simple and knowable. The Bible counselor knows the solutions to bitterness, anger, alcoholism, drug addictions, sexual perversions, lust, marriage failure—you name it. We know the steps: the one, two, three's. The academics are not only easy, they are simple. So what is the problem? It's a bondage at the core level that disempowers people from following the steps.

In this passage, the "son of man" is the counselor. God is telling the son of man, the counsellor, what to tell them:

*"Therefore speak unto them,*
*and say unto them,*
*Thus saith the Lord GOD . . ."*

God intends to tell the real truth, the real solution, and do so directly; some of the prophets, the counselors, are not going to give the right answers, because the answers are not politically correct, not in vogue, not sophisticated enough for the culture. They are too religious, too "off the beaten path" of mainstream psychology. Here's God speaking:

*"Every man . . . that setteth up his idols in his heart,*
*and **putteth the stumblingblock of his iniquity before his face**,*
*and cometh to the prophet;*
*I the LORD will answer him that cometh*
*according to the multitude of his idols."*
(Ezekiel 14:4)

God calls the issue, "idols set up because of the stumblingblock of iniquity." Iniquity is the self-determination of pursuits based on the perception of what will gratify and satiate the ruling false god of ego; however, this god does not possess the intelligence, the wisdom, or the character to be God. Man is egocentric instead of theocentric; self-centered instead of God-centered. The problem is the person who is smack dab in the middle of the word sIn, the center of the word prIde, and occurs three times in the word InIquIty. This unconverted "I" decides on idols, sins, abominations, and then enquires help from God. But God says:

*". . . they are all estranged from me through their idols.*
*. . . Thus saith the Lord GOD;*

*Repent, and turn yourselves from your idols;*
*and turn away your faces from all your abominations."*
(Ezekiel 14:5-6)

All men without God are in desperate trouble. Men without God are estranged; they are turned away to other controlling powers; they are turned to their idols; they are turned to those persons, places, things, or behaviors that they themselves have set up. Man has purposely separated himself from God. The answer is to repent, to turn away from, and to destroy those idols and abominations.

*". . . which separateth himself from me,*
*and setteth up his idols in his heart,*
*and **putteth the stumblingblock of his iniquity***
***before his face**, and cometh to a prophet*
*to enquire of him concerning me;*
*I the LORD will answer him by myself:*
*And I will set my face against that man . . ."*
(Ezekiel 14:7-8)

The prophet, the counselor, doesn't have the option whether to draw the line or not to draw the line. No option is given by God to the counselor no matter how well-meaning he or she may be. God says it won't work. Destruction is sure. The only answer to prevent failure is to 1) repent; 2) turn from the idols; 3) turn from abominations; 4) get rid of the stumbling block of iniquity.

If the prophet or Christian counselor does not deal with the matter, the consequences are quite severe, because to the counselor, the failure to deal with this becomes his iniquity.

> *"And they (the Prophet or the Counsellor)*
> *shall bear the punishment of their iniquity:*
> *the punishment of the prophet shall be*
> *even as the punishment of him that seeketh unto him."*
> (Ezekiel 14:10)

Beloved, this is a fearful thing. To stand before Almighty God and be accountable to Him for the directions we give to those within our sphere of influence. James warned us, *"My brethren, be not many masters, knowing that we shall receive the greater condemnation"* (James 3:1). The word *"masters"* refers to instructors or teachers.

In my office, the first counselling session has only one subject: Whose will are you intending to follow? Yours or God's? I simply don't have time to describe the wonders of God's ways to those who have no intention of following them. I press it pretty hard. Uncomfortably so, at times. And that is precisely when the *"spirit of might"* is so necessary. In my natural self, I would rather smile and hand out some nice spiritual platitudes and be thought of as a nice pastor, an accommodating counselor. But the fear of God demands otherwise.

God's ways are easy, but only to those who've given up the throne of their hearts—the control center and management position—to the only One wise enough and loving enough to lead, guide, and direct. To the transgressor God's ways are hard, because they cut across the grain of every false pursuit, every wickedness, every abomination, every way contrary to genuine love. Those who insist on keeping the stumbling block of iniquity before their face cannot, I repeat, cannot, be helped. Thereby, they have separated themselves from God. Failure is the consequence. Weep over them! I say, weep over them! But compromise, never!

## 12. Iniquity must be dealt with.

Ignoring iniquity is not an option. It is as damning and damaging in its consequences as any evil or wickedness, for it is indeed the fountain of all such. Of all people, we, as Christians in particular, should be delivered. As we shall see, deliverance from iniquity is the motive, the reason, the cause, the power, and the ability of the Savior. But we must do our part as well. Never forget the adage: Without God, we cannot. Without us, He will not.

> *"Let every one that nameth the name of Christ*
> *depart from **iniquity**."*
> (2 Timothy 2:19)

## CHAPTER SIX

# The Effects of Iniquity on Family Life

*"If thou return to the Almighty, thou shalt be built up,*
*thou shalt put away iniquity far from thy tabernacles."*
(Job 22:23)

**1. Iniquities can be inherited.**

Although we have alluded to this above, it ought to be noted that not only do the consequences of the iniquities of the fathers (not the mothers) affect subsequent generations of children, but some of the iniquities of the fathers are actually transferable to the children. Nowhere in Scripture are we taught that sin is transferable. Sin is a wrong moral act, a transgression of a law. The consequences of a sin may affect others, but the sin itself is not transferred—neither in the blood stream, nor by any other mechanism. Some sects forbid blood transfusions because of this false reasoning. They think sin is in the blood and therefore would be transferred. The Scripture says, *"The fathers shall not die for the children, neither shall the children die for the fathers, but every man shall die for his own sin"* (2 Chronicles 25:4). Again, we will deal more fully with this issue in a later chapter. In the meantime note the following:

*"... for I the LORD thy God am a jealous God,*
*visiting **the iniquity of the fathers** upon the children*
*unto the third and fourth generation of them that hate me;*

*And shewing mercy unto thousands of them*
*that love me, and keep my commandments."*
(Exodus 20:5-6)

## 2. Iniquity destroys homes.

Our homes, like our churches, ought to be the safest places in the world: a sanctuary for all who gather there. But a home full of iniquity is a dangerous training ground. The home is the classroom of life. The lessons are learned by example and instruction. A boy learns how to treat women by observing how his father treats his wife, the boy's mother. A girl learns how to respond to a husband by observing her mother's response to her husband, the girl's father. Equity is learned in the home when the husband and father loves his wife, the mother of his children, like Christ loves His church.

Turning to God and His ways is the first step to the establishment of the home. Putting away iniquity from our dwelling places is the second. Discipline is the third. Note this in these Scriptures:

*"If thou return to the Almighty, thou shalt be built up,*
*thou shalt **put away iniquity far from thy tabernacles**."*
(Job 22:23)

*"He openeth also their ear to discipline,*
*and commandeth that they return from **iniquity**.*
*If they obey and serve him,*

*they shall spend their days in prosperity,*
*and their years in pleasures."*
(Job 36:10-11)

## 3. Iniquity causes divorce.

I tell my wife, "If you ever leave me, I'm going with you." One of the biggest tests of life is marriage. It's really a test of love. Before marriage, most of us were looking for a "good deal." Our basis of interest in the other person was what we could get out of it. This is the agenda of iniquity. The system of dating is so flawed, which is one of the reasons I stopped teaching on the subject. We "try people out" and then usually leave a trail of discards behind us. Or we become one of the discards. The spiritual, mental, emotional, and social effects of being tried out and then trashed cannot be over-estimated. It can leave us with life-long wounds that never heal. The motive for dating is what can we get out of it, instead of what can we give. Genuine love is about giving to others without personal profit as a motive.

As an alternative to the try-before-you-buy philosophy we attempt to turn relationships into a negotiation. If you do this, I'll do that. One way or another, most of us end up at the marriage altar. Instead, marriage should be based on the will of God, on love, on vows, and the realization that together we can be more effective for God than if we were separate.

At the marriage, the preacher begins, "Dearly Beloved, we are here gathered together in the sight of God, and you who are witnesses, to join together this man and this woman in the bonds of holy matrimony." He proceeds, "Marriage is not to be entered into lightly nor thoughtlessly but soberly, reverently, and in the fear of the Lord."

In the fear of the Lord? How so? To answer that, we must understand that the vows are being made before El Shaddai, the Lord God Almighty. How fearful ought that to be? Here is how fearful:

*"Be not rash with thy mouth,*
*and let not thine heart be hasty*
*to utter any thing before God:*
*for God is in heaven, and thou upon earth:*
*therefore let thy words be few.*

*When thou vowest a vow unto God,*
*defer not to pay it;*
*for he hath no pleasure in fools:*
*pay that which thou hast vowed.*

*Better is it that thou shouldest not vow,*
*than that thou shouldest vow and not pay."*

Iniquity is not living equal to our vows. And God gives no leniency to ignorance. Not keeping vows made before God is playing the fool, yea, establishing ourselves as fools. Ouch! Ouch! Ouch! But the warnings go on:

*"Suffer not thy mouth to cause thy flesh to sin;*
*neither say thou before the angel,*
*that it was an error:*
*wherefore should God be angry at thy voice,*
*and destroy the work of thine hands?"*
(Ecclesiastes 5:2-6)

Notice! We don't get to say it was a mistake, an error. If we do, God will be angry and destroy the work of our hands. Our employment and our finances will be damaged. God watches marriages. God watches how husbands treat wives and how wives treat husbands. And He expects us to treat one another in keeping with the vows we made before heaven and earth.

Now let's get the details from Scripture and see in black and white that the mistreatment of a spouse is iniquity. First, we see the standard for God's representatives:

*"My covenant was with him of life and peace;*
*and I gave them to him for the fear*
*wherewith he feared me,*
*and was afraid before my name.*

*The law of truth was in his mouth,*
*and **iniquity** was not found in his lips:*
*he walked with me in peace and **equity**,*
*and did turn many away from **iniquity**.*

*For the priest's lips should keep knowledge,*
*and they should seek the law at his mouth:*
*for he is the messenger of the LORD of hosts. "*
(Malachi 2:5-7)

Notice: 1) the minister had a covenant with God; 2) The minister had the fear of God; 3) The minister told the truth; 4) The minister spoke no iniquity; 5) The minister walked in peace and equity, the opposite to iniquity; 6) The mission was to turn others away from iniquity; 7) The minister was to possess knowledge and know the laws of God; and 8) He was to accurately represent His Lord.

However, in Malachi, the above standards were not followed. In fact they had so departed from the ways of the Lord that they had become treacherous with one another, had profaned the holiness of the Lord, and ended up cut off from the Lord.

They would cry and give offerings to the Lord, but God rejected their tears and their offerings. You are about to see why:

*"And this have ye done again,*
*covering the altar of the LORD with tears,*
*with weeping, and with crying out,*
*insomuch that he regardeth not the offering any more,*
*or receiveth it with good will at your hand.*

> *Yet ye say, Wherefore?*
> *Because the LORD hath been witness*
> *between thee and the wife of thy youth,*
> *against whom thou hast dealt treacherously:*
> *yet is she thy companion, and the wife of thy covenant."*
> (Malachi 2:13-14)

Why did God not respond to their tears? Why did God reject their offerings? Why did God not receive their goodness? Because they had dealt treacherously with their wives. Yet God's reasons go even beyond that. It was because dealing treacherously with wives damages the children. He made the man and wife to be one. Why? Because God wants Godly children and treachery between a husband and wife destroys that. Take a look:

> *"And did not he make one*
> *Yet had he the residue of the spirit.*
> *And wherefore one?*
> *That he might seek a godly seed.*
> *Therefore take heed to your spirit,*
> *and let none deal treacherously*
> *against the wife of his youth."*
> (Malachi 2:15)

Treachery is secretly doing harmful things to someone who trusts you. It is a violation of loyalty and allegiance, a breaking of confidence and faith. Let's cut to the core, the nasty truth about iniquity: it causes treachery, the putting away of one's spouse (divorce), and violence.

> *For the LORD, the God of Israel,*
> *saith that he hateth putting away:*
> *for one covereth violence with his garment,*
> *saith the LORD of hosts:*
> *therefore take heed to your spirit,*
> *that ye deal not treacherously."*
> (Malachi 2:16)

Divorce is a violent act. But we treacherous men (and perhaps women) try to cover up the violence of it like covering a dagger with a coat. We pretend it can be done in a friendly fashion. But the dagger still cuts and twists, and wounds and damages. It might be better if it were only flesh wounds, wounds that could heal, but they are soul wounds, yea they are, according to these Scriptures, *spirit wounds*. Thus the warning, *"take heed to your spirit."* The wounding of a person's spirit is far worse than mental and emotional damage, worse than physical damage.

> *"The spirit of a man will sustain his infirmity;*
> *but a wounded spirit who can bear?*
> (Proverbs 18:14)

Notice the reasons God hates divorce. They are taken from the above passages:

1) Treacherous dealing
2) Fake crying at the altars
3) Gifts given to God as bribes
4) No good will
5) Deserting of a companion
6) Breaking of covenant
7) Damaging of children which He has made

What's at the root of divorce? Iniquity!

> *"Thus saith the LORD,*
> *Where is the bill of your mother's divorcement,*
> *whom I have put away?*
> *or which of my creditors is it to whom I have sold you?*
> *Behold, **for your iniquities have ye sold yourselves**,*
> *and for your transgressions is your mother put away."*
> (Isaiah 50:1)

*"Ye have wearied the LORD with your words.*
*Yet ye say, Wherein have we wearied him?*
*When ye say, Every one that doeth evil is good*
*in the sight of the LORD,*
*and he delighteth in them; or,*
*Where is the God of judgment?"*
(Malachi 2:17)

The ultimate iniquity is saying that evil is good in the sight of the Lord, and to add insult to injury, to say that the Lord takes delight in this iniquity—this evil—or that He doesn't care. Ouch! Ouch! Ouch!

Marriage is a spiritual union. Intercourse is a spiritual act. It affects covenant. And all of this is the fruit of iniquity.

### 4. Iniquity causes a lack of restraint with children.

Children are trained in iniquity by untrained parents. Duties! We have a lot of them, and none as great as that of being a father. Equity, the opposite of iniquity, means that a father must be equal to his task; he must do his fatherly duties. Not to do so is iniquity. Raising the children is not Mom's job. It's Dad's. *"Ye fathers, provoke not your children to wrath: but bring them up in the nurture and admonition of the Lord"* (Ephesians 6:4). *"Bring them up"* is the command to fathers, not mothers. We don't get to desert the ship or shirk this task. To do so is iniquity. The proof is found in 1 Samuel.

Eli was a priest, and little Samuel was dedicated by his parents to the Lord and thus served Eli. Now watch this wonderful insight: *"And the word of the Lord was precious in those days"* (1 Samuel 3:1). However, Eli had sons, and like all sons, they needed discipline and correction. But he did not restrain them; that is a form of iniquity. Notice that this particular kind of iniquity has long-range, devastating consequences which are multi-generational:

*"For I have told him that I will judge his house for ever*
*for **the iniquity which he knoweth**;*
*because his sons made themselves vile,*
*and he restrained them not."*
(1 Samuel 3:13)

His iniquity was that he did not restrain his sons.

It gets worse. Remember, *". . . the iniquities of the fathers,"* not the *sins* of the fathers, *"shall be visited upon the children to the third and fourth generation . . ."* (Exodus 20:5 & 34:7). We will spend a whole chapter on how to overcome the iniquities of our fathers, but in the case of Eli, such iniquity could not be reversed:

*"And therefore I have sworn unto the house of Eli,*
*that the iniquity of Eli's house shall not be purged*
*with sacrifice nor offering for ever."*
(1 Samuel 3:14)

# CHAPTER SEVEN

# The Effects of Iniquity on Society

*"...their thoughts are thoughts of iniquity:*
*wasting and destruction are in their paths."*
(Isaiah 59:7)

## 1. Iniquity is the cause of all crime.

Can you think of any crime that is not directly caused by iniquity? There are 240 *"thou shalt nots"* in the Bible. Each one of them intended to lovingly prevent some form of iniquity. Ten of them are the most famous. Our culture seems anxious to do away with them, because they interfere with the accelerated desire to have iniquity unrestrained. The western culture seems bent on decriminalizing items which have long been deemed as crimes and violations of civilized norms. *"Thou shalt not commit adultery,"* is taken out of the schools, and the courts and society in general. *"Thou shalt not covet,"* is certainly not in vogue. In fact the advertising industry is based on creating desires, even artificially, to sell products. People will not buy what they do not first covet.

We have become a society obsessed with selfish pursuits that surpass the guarantees of our founding documents, which enunciate "liberty and justice for all." We've forgotten that our freedom ends where another person's nose begins, and we feed upon one another like vultures. Liberty can only function where there is love, the opposite of iniquity.

> *". . . ye have been called unto liberty;*
> *only use not liberty for an occasion to the flesh,*
> *but by love serve one another.*
> *For all the law is fulfilled in one word, even in this;*
> *Thou shalt love thy neighbour as thyself.*
> ***But if ye bite and devour one another***
> ***take heed that ye be not consumed one of another."***
> (Galatians 5:13-15)

The misuse of liberty and the contest of wills must end, or it will continue to impel us toward anarchy, the state of disorder described in Scripture as, *"every man did that which was right in his own eyes"* (Judges 17:6). It seems to me that whatever is immoral ought also to be illegal.

The Bible commands, *"Thou shalt not kill."* Murder is an ultimate form of iniquity, the taking of another's life without moral or legal cause. We kill babies with impunity. The value of human life is dropping in our culture. One hundred feet from my home you can be fined up to $10,000 or imprisoned for killing turtles before they are born, but there is no penalty for taking a human life through abortion.

Murder is a severe iniquity but the ultimate God-playing act is suicide, or self-murder. The CDC (Centers For Disease Control and Prevention) collects data about mortality in the United States, including deaths by suicide. The AFSP (American Foundation For Suicide Prevention) reports this data: "In 2013, there were 41,149 suicides reported, making suicide the tenth leading cause of death for Americans. In that year, someone in this country died by suicide every 12.8 minutes" (afsp.org).

## 2. Iniquity corrupts the judicial system.

God is superlatively interested in justice. Without justice the whole universe would become as an unguarded and uncontrolled prison. It must be settled in our thinking that justice is not only an interest of God, but a responsibility, and he is up to the task: *"Justice and judgment are the habitation of thy throne"* (Psalm 89:14). Job said it clearly: *"Touching the Almighty, we cannot find him out: he is excellent in power, and in judgment, and in plenty of justice . . ."* (Job 37:23).

Justice is such a high a priority with God that the Scriptures declare, *"To do justice and judgment is more acceptable to the LORD than sacrifice"* (Proverbs 21:3).

> *"And moreover I saw under the sun*
> *the place of judgment, that wickedness was there;*
> *and the place of righteousness,*
> *that **iniquity** was there."*
> (Ecclesiastes 3:16)

You can see the shocking accusation that in the place where there should be proper legal adjudications and the doing of right, both wickedness and iniquity are present.

In an iniquitous culture, justice is wanting. In Isaiah's day it was this way: *"None calleth for justice, nor any pleadeth for truth: they trust in vanity, and speak lies; they conceive mischief, and bring forth iniquity"* (Isaiah 59:4). Be sure to notice the connection between the lack of justice and iniquity. The description goes further: *"And judgment is turned away backward, and justice standeth afar off: for truth is fallen in the street, and **equity** cannot enter"* (Isaiah 59:14). Note *"equity cannot enter."* This is simply a restatement of iniquity: the lack of equity.

Understanding the relationship between iniquity and the lack of justice is so vital; I want you to see it clearly and in more detail. As you read, take note of the numerous characteristics of iniquity:

"... *their thoughts are thoughts of iniquity;*
*wasting and destruction are in their paths.*

*The way of peace they know not;*
*and there is no judgment in their goings:*
*they have made them crooked paths:*
*whosoever goeth therein shall not know peace.*

*Therefore is judgment far from us,*
*neither doth justice overtake us:*
*we wait for light, but behold obscurity*
*for brightness, but we walk in darkness.*

*We grope for the wall like the blind,*
*and we grope as if we had no eyes:*
*we stumble at noonday as in the night*
*we are in desolate places as dead men.*

*We roar all like bears, and mourn sore like doves:*
*we look for judgment, but there is none;*
*for salvation, but it is far off from us.*

*For our transgressions are multiplied before thee,*
*and our sins testify against us:*
*for our transgressions are with us;*
*and as for our **iniquities**, we know them;"*
(Isaiah 59:7-12)

If you were God, and held justice in high esteem, what would you do about assuring justice on the planet; in each culture; in each country, state, or providence; in each county, city, town, or village? God's answer was, and is, to decree the terms of each judicial system. God establishes a minimum requirement for those filling the judicial position of *judge*.

Just adjudications are to be made by qualified men and/or women. We are going to look at the details of these qualifications, but before we do, there is one more point of clarification needed.

Throughout the Scriptures, frequent references are made to *"gods"* with a lowercase "g." Sometimes this refers to idols or false gods, who are actually no gods at all. They are, *". . . the work of men's hands. They have mouths, but they speak not; eyes have they, but they see not; They have ears, but they hear not; neither is there any breath in their mouths. They that make them are like unto them: so is every one that trusteth in them"* (Psalm 135:15-18).

Most frequently, and more legitimately, the term *"gods"* refers to judges: the key players in the judicial system. The reason they are referred to as gods is because they are to be the earthly representatives of God Himself, exercising justice on behalf of the Almighty. Judges aren't to act on behalf of men, but on behalf of God.

> *"And said to the judges, Take heed what ye do:*
> *for ye judge not for man,*
> *but for the LORD, who is with you in the judgment.*
>
> *Wherefore now let the fear of the LORD be upon you;*
> *take heed and do it:*
> *for there is no iniquity with the LORD our God,*
> *nor respect of persons, nor taking of gifts."*
> (2 Chronicles 19:6-7)

Notice the crucial elements, the critical qualifications, and the vital requirements for judges:

1) They must take heed (give extreme attention).

2) They must judge on behalf of God, as His representative.

3) They must count on God for help.

4) They must have the fear of God.

5) They must have the absence of iniquity.

6) They must show *"no respect of persons"* (no favoritism).

7) They must not take gifts (no self-benefit).

## 3. Iniquity is the cause of racism.

Racism is the assertion that one race is superior to another. The cry for social justice can be heard in our land. It is the view that everyone deserves equal economic, political, and social rights. It does not mean that equal outcomes will be achieved in a given society.

But equal opportunity can be thwarted by racial discrimination. It is iniquity that causes prejudice, discrimination, and antagonism directed toward those of a different race. The *"one-blood"* principle of the Scriptures are clear:

> *"And He hath made of one blood all nations of men*
> *for to dwell on all the face of the earth . . ."*
> (Acts 17:26)

Xenophobia, an irrational fear or hatred of foreigners, is a by-product of racism. How we are to treat the foreigner, the stranger in our land, is not optional to true followers of the Lord. And let us never forget that America was founded and perpetuated on Scriptural principles. The American attitude was birthed from the Scriptures:

> *"And if a stranger sojourn with thee in your land,*
> *ye shall not vex him.*

*But the stranger that dwelleth with you*
*shall be unto you as one born among you,*
*and thou shalt love him as thyself;*
*for ye were strangers in the land of Egypt:*
*I am the LORD your God."*
(Leviticus 19:33-34)

It is no wonder that "in New York Harbor there stands a lady with a torch raised to the sky." She is aptly called, "The Mother of Exiles," a gift of friendship from the people of France, dedicated on October 28, 1886. The Statute of Liberty is a colossal neoclassical sculpture on Ellis Island, the historic welcoming entrance to immigrants. The Lady bears the inscription, a sonnet. It reads:

Not like the brazen giant of Greek fame,
With conquering limbs astride from land to land;
Here at our sea-washed, sunset gates shall stand
A mighty woman with a torch, whose flame
Is the imprisoned lightning, and her name
Mother of Exiles. From her beacon-hand
Glows world-wide welcome; her mild eyes command
The air-bridged harbor that twin cities frame.
"Keep, ancient lands, your storied pomp!" cries she
With silent lips. "Give me your tired, your poor,
Your huddled masses yearning to breathe free,
The wretched refuse of your teeming shore.
Send these, the homeless, tempest-tossed to me,
I lift my lamp beside the golden door!

This is the real America as she was designed to be. And we do well to give thanks to Martin Luther King, Jr., for leading us back to civility, back to the recovery of forgotten and transgressed principles.

The iniquity of racism is one of the greatest problems of the world, whether it be Arab versus Jew, Black versus White, or any ethnos against another ethnos. This iniquity is spelled w-a-r.

## 4. Iniquity is the cause of gender inequality.

A woman is a *wombed* man. For centuries, however, she was mistreated as a beast of burden, an object to be purchased as an asset, or to be disposed of as a liability. In respect to the value of women, misrepresentations of the Scriptures abound. Are women equal with men? That is the question. Certainly it should be plain that men and women are equal in value, though different in function. For example, I don't suspect that men will ever give birth to babies. Men are not equal to that task. Someone said that if it was ever the man's job to give birth to a baby, there would only be one baby.

A contest between genders has been going on forever and sometimes quite humorously. Someone sent me a story about a store in Miami that was selling husbands. A woman may go to choose a husband from among many men. The store is comprised of six floors and the men increase in positive attributes as the shopper ascends the different levels of the floor. There is, however, a catch: as you open the door to any floor, you may choose any man from that floor; but if you go up a floor, you cannot go back down, except to exit the building. So a woman goes to the shopping center to find a husband and the sign on the door reads *Floor #1 - These men have jobs*. So she reads the sign and says, "Well that's better than my last boyfriend, but I'm wondering what's farther up." So she goes to the second floor, and the second floor sign reads *Floor 2 - These men have jobs and love kids*. So the woman remarks to herself, "Boy, that's great, but I wonder what's farther up." And up she goes again, and the third floor sign reads *Floor 3 - These men have jobs, love kids and are extremely good looking*. She thinks that sounds good but wonders what is upstairs. The fourth sign reads *Floor 4 - These men have jobs, love kids, are good looking, and help with the house work.* "Wow!" exclaims the woman. "It's very tempting, but there must be more." So again she heads up another flight of stairs, to the fifth floor, and the sign reads *Floor 5 - These men have jobs, love kids, are good looking, do house work, and have a strong romantic streak.* And the woman says, "What could be waiting for me farther up!" So up to the sixth floor she goes, and the sign reads *Floor 6 - You are visitor 3,456,789 to this floor. There are no men on this floor. This floor exists solely to prove that women are impossible to please. Thank you for shopping at Husband Mart.*

Hey, guys, don't get smug. The roles could easily have been reversed. It could have been a store that sells wives. Admit it, you probably would have done the same thing.

Why this contest between men and women? Why has such an undignified, warped, and twisted disparity existed for centuries? The only answer I know is iniquity, the raising up of one and the putting down of another, not accepting the par. As Peter Marshall said it so accurately, and so eloquently, "The emancipation of womanhood began with Christianity, and it ends with Christianity. It had its beginning one night two thousand years ago when there came to a woman named Mary a vision and a message from heaven. She saw the rifted clouds of glory and the hidden battlements of heaven. She heard an angelic annunciation of the almost incredible news that she, of all the women on earth—of all the Marys in history—was to be the only one who should ever wear entwined the red rose of maternity and the white rose of virginity."

Mary did more for womanhood than any woman in history. She gave birth to the Son of God, and God the Son. For centuries since, womanhood has been the subject of the poet's pen and the artist's brush. Mixing paint and pigment on canvas, they have tried to capture the character of her countenance, the essence of her beauty, and the dignity of her gender.

When Napoleon Bonaparte was asked what he considered to be the great need of France, he replied, "Good mothers." It was William Ross Wallace (1819-1881) who wrote the poem titled "The Hand That Rocks The Cradle Is The Hand That Rules The World," some lines of which were mistakenly accredited to Napoleon. So valuable is it, that I include it in its entirety.

BLESSINGS on the hand of women!
Angels guard its strength and grace.
In the palace, cottage, hovel,
Oh, no matter where the place;
Would that never storms assailed it,
Rainbows ever gently curled,
For the hand that rocks the cradle
Is the hand that rules the world.

Infancy's the tender fountain,
Power may with beauty flow,
Mothers first to guide the streamlets,
From them souls unresting grow—
Grow on for the good or evil,
Sunshine streamed or evil hurled,
For the hand that rocks the cradle
Is the hand that rules the world.

Woman, how divine your mission,
Here upon our natal sod;
Keep—oh, keep the young heart open
Always to the breath of God!
All true trophies of the ages

Are from mother-love impearled,
For the hand that rocks the cradle
Is the hand that rules the world.

Blessings on the hand of women!
Fathers, sons, and daughters cry,
And the sacred song is mingled
With the worship in the sky—
Mingles where no tempest darkens,
Rainbows evermore are hurled;
For the hand that rocks the cradle
Is the hand that rules the world.

Perhaps it is not women that need to be brought up to the level of men but rather that men should be brought up to the level of true womanhood. Let's all of us, both genders, strive to be what we should be. Let's all get out of the gutters. Peter Marshall said, "We need women, and men, too, who would rather be morally right than socially correct."

## 5. Iniquity must ultimately be confined and/or destroyed.

God cannot, will not, and must not give eternal life to iniquity. Can you imagine a universe where iniquity is eternalized, supernaturally endowed and allowed to function unrestrained? That is what hell is. Hell is at the end of a self-serving life, where the character qualities that we have chosen and developed become permanent. In the meantime, sin and iniquity are allowed to be mixed in with normality.

Jesus tells us that the wheat and the tares, the genuine and the hypocritical, must be allowed to grow together. The tares look just like the wheat. Hypocrites and Christians look a lot alike. It's hard to detect a hypocrite. But they must be allowed to grow together, to attend the same churches, to act out the same religious rituals. Jesus said that to attempt pulling the tares and separating them, one would risk damage to the wheat, so let them be . . . for now. But:

*"The harvest is the end of the world;*
*and the reapers are the angels.*

*As therefore the tares are gathered*
*and burned in the fire;*
*so shall it be in the end of this world.*

*The Son of man shall send forth his angels,*
*and they shall gather out of his kingdom*
*all things that offend,*
*and **them which do iniquity**;*

*And shall cast them into a furnace of fire:*
*there shall be wailing and gnashing of teeth.*

*Then shall the righteous shine forth*
*as the sun in the kingdom of their Father.*
*Who hath ears to hear, let him hear."*
(Matthew 13:39-43)

Who are the tares? Those that do iniquity!

## 6. Iniquity has a cure, a solution, a resolution.

It is found in Christ, and in Christ alone. It will be my endeavor to articulate God's adequate redemption from the condition of iniquity. Pray along as you read. My dearest hope is that with God's help you will experience a wonderful, life-freeing reality. No exaggerations here. You will be able to say with the Psalmist, *"Our soul is escaped as a bird out of the snare of the fowlers: the snare is broken, and we are escaped"* (Psalm 124:7).

For the moment, however, it is sufficed to cite a Scripture for your confidence:

*"Unto you first God,*
*having raised up his Son Jesus,*
*sent him **to bless you,***
***in turning away every one of you***
***from his iniquities."***
(Acts 3:26)

This is the first and finest intention of God. He will do it because His Son, Jesus, was resurrected for this purpose. You will be blessed by this turning away. You are included in the *"every one of you."* Your iniquities will be gone.

# CHAPTER EIGHT

# Iniquity: The Power Behind Sin

*"By this therefore shall*
*the iniquity of Jacob be purged;*
*and this is all the fruit to take away his sin . . ."*
(Isaiah 27:9)

*"And I will cleanse them from*
*all their iniquity, whereby they have*
*sinned against me;*
*and I will pardon all their iniquities,*
*whereby they have sinned,*
*and whereby they have*
*transgressed against me.*

*And it shall be to me a name of joy,*
*a praise and an honour*
*before all the nations of the earth . . ."*
(Jeremiah 33:8-9)

Why is the propensity to sin so strong, so fervent, and sometimes even violent? Why does it seem that we cannot stop sinning? Is it just the power of habit? Paul described it this way, *"I find then a law, that, when I would do good, evil is present with me"* (Romans 7:21). He said he wanted to do good but went on to explain, *"But I see another law in my members, warring against the law of my mind, and bringing me into captivity to the law of sin which is in my members"* (Romans 7:23). What is this power behind sin? The answer is iniquity. Here's the Biblical evidence:

> *"And I will cleanse them from all their **iniquity,***
> ***whereby they have sinned** against me;*
> *and I will pardon all their **iniquities,***
> ***whereby they have sinned,** and*
> ***whereby** they have transgressed against me."*
> (Jeremiah 33:8)

Note the cause and effect assertions of the Scripture: *"iniquity whereby they have sinned,"* (cited twice for emphasis), and *"whereby they have transgressed."* Iniquity is the energy, the motive, the active and forceful dynamic driving us to sins—sins of every diverse sort. Here are several examples:

**Sexual Sins**

In Ephesians chapter six, we find he Christian's Armor listed. Twice we are admonished, *"Put on the whole armour of God."* The first time, it is so that we *"may be able to stand against the wiles of the devil."* The second time, it is so we *"may be able to withstand in the evil day, and having done all, to stand."*

How unfortunate that accurate instruction of this passage is so scarce. For example, the first piece of armor we are to put on is about one's sexuality: *"Stand therefore, having your loins girt about with truth."* The very first piece of armor is designed to protect one's loins, one's reproductive parts: one's sexuality.

The allegory of wearing armor in a battle tells us how important, yea, how imperative it is to have protection. And this first essential is protection for your private parts. So what is this armor made of, and how do you put it on so that you will not be defeated by Satan in this area? How do you put on this vital piece of armor so that you can withstand the evils—the sensual and sexual evils—of our day?

I've heard preachers recommend standing in front of your mirror in the morning and going through the motions of donning your equipment. How mystical and how superstitious is that? Now you'd be going out unprotected but thinking that you are protected. Very dangerous. The Scriptures say that the armor that is designed to protect your sacred parts is *truth*. But what truth? It surely doesn't mean the whole Bible of truth. It must be specific truth because later on we are to take, *"the sword of the Spirit, which is the Word of God."* The Word of God is the whole truth. The truths that are needed to protect your loins are the truths in the Bible about sexuality. They are found in Proverbs chapters 5, 6, 7, 9, and 23:26-28; 1 Thessalonians 4:1-8; 1 Corinthians 7:1-10; and 2 Timothy 2:22.

How do you put the armor on? How do you know you're wearing it, that you have it with you? The answer is by memorizing those truths about sexuality. Now they will speak to you, advise you, and empower you every time you need them. For example, let's say you've memorized Proverbs 23:27, *"For a whore is a deep ditch; and a strange woman is a narrow pit."* Or in The Message translation of the Bible, it reads, *"A whore is a bottomless pit; a loose woman can get you in trouble real fast. She'll take you for all you've got; she is worse than a pack of thieves."* Now when you meet a sensual looking girl, that verse will click in and give you warning. Watch out! Instead of running to the slaughter like a fool, you will act with this Scripture in mind.

You have on the armor to protect your loins when you have memorized the passages of Scriptural truths about sexuality as listed above.

What does iniquity have to do with sexuality?

We are asked this question: *"And why wilt thou, my son, be ravished with a strange woman, and embrace the bosom of a stranger?"* (Proverbs 5:20). Two verses later it explains that this is iniquity, and it explains that this iniquity causes sin, destruction, and folly:

*"His own **iniquities** shall take the wicked himself,*
*and he shall be holden with the cords of his sins.*

*He shall die without instruction;*
*and in the greatness of his folly he shall go astray."*
(Proverbs 5:22-23)

Iniquity creates desires to take what is not ours. And when it comes to sexuality, iniquity is a monster. In the following passage about impurity, immorality, and unlawful sexuality we find the description of the thirst of iniquity:

*"Stolen waters are sweet,*
*and bread eaten in secret is pleasant.*

*But he knoweth not that the dead are there;*
*and that her guests are in the depths of hell."*
(Proverbs 9:17-18)

Iniquity desires stolen waters. By the way, in the Appendix you will find several keys to understanding sexuality in the King James Version of Proverbs. Don't be mistaken. God addresses very real life issues, but He does it in a dignified way. Our culture has become so crass about sexual things that we often don't understand the meanings when they are presented modestly.

In Leviticus chapter twenty, we learn that viewing the nakedness of others, even one's own parent or sibling is both a wicked thing and an iniquity. (See Leviticus 20:17, 19)

## Eating Disorders

Iniquity, as you have learned, affects every aspect of life. It should not come as a surprise that iniquity seeks to drive our eating habits and manifests itself in several ways:

1. Eating for recreation instead of for nutrition.
2. Eating for pleasure instead of eating for health.
3. Eating more than we should, leading to obesity and gluttony.

4.  Eating less than we should, leading to anorexia, the leading cause of death among young women age 15-24.

## Self-Acceptance

Iniquity pushes us to want to be something or someone we are not. Iniquity causes rivalry. It causes one-upmanship, competition, and the comparison of ourselves with others. Oh, the horrors of thinking we are less than others. And we do this even when it is not true. So we compete, we attempt to outdo, we outperform, and we out-show everyone else. Then there are some who realize the vanity of it all and drop out, cop-out, give up, and turn to self-destructive behaviors. Iniquity is at the root of non-self-acceptance. Life is not meant to be a rat race; a competition with everyone else.

How can we be happy, truly happy, with ourselves? When we realize that God made us, and He makes no junk. He has a design and purpose for our lives and for our after-life. True joy bursts from us when we realize this. I am a somebody, a wonderful *somebody*. Once this truth grips a person's thinking, they will be careful not to spoil what He has made them to be. An old adage which originated with Hans Urs von Balthasar, the Swiss Jesuit Philosopher, says:

"What you are is God's gift to you.
What you become is your gift to God."

## Money

Someone said, "The lottery is the punishment of those who failed math." Do you know the history of lottery winners? I'll let you look up the details. But you will find in their path a consistent horrid wake of suicide, debt, bankruptcy, prison, abuse, divorce, hatred, murder, and brokenness. Everyone says, "If I won, I would be different. I would know how to use the money wisely." They usually follow up the statement with "I'd give . . ." Then when the charitable "front" has seemingly convinced you how unselfish they are, they proceed with a tirade of "I would" statements.

But why the almost unbroken pattern of destruction demonstrated by their history? Perhaps the Scriptures should once again be consulted:

> *"A faithful man shall abound with blessings:*
> *But he that maketh hast to be rich*
> *Shall not be innocent."*
> (Proverbs 28:20)

> *"He that hasteth to be rich*
> *hath an evil eye.*
> *And conidereth not that*
> *Poverty shall come upon him."*
> (Proverbs 28:22)

There are a thousand ways to poverty, but only two ways to riches. The two ways to riches are God's way and man's way. However, the end result is not the same. God's way to riches makes you rich, but there are "no sorrows" with it. It's a principle based way. Man's way can make you rich, but oh, the sorrows that come with it: debt, broken health, destroyed marriages and friendships, maybe even jail time. Ask Bernie Madoff. Man's way, is the way of iniquity.

> *"The blessing of the LORD, it maketh rich,*
> *and he addeth no sorrow with it. "*
> (Proverbs 10:22)

When it comes to money and the use of assets, iniquity is negatively impacting because it prevents "principle based" decision making.

### The Philosophic Core

Iniquity has, at its core, a philosophy. It would be accurate to say that iniquity consists of a core philosophy. In fact, iniquity is a philosophy! But I don't want to spoil you simply by telling it to you. Having read this far in the book (and for that you should receive congratulations – you've proven that you are a thinking, conscientious person), you should be able to detect iniquity quite easily. So

I'm going to test you. Let's see if you can pick out the philosophy of iniquity in the following passage. Here's the setting: Jesus is calling for disciples, real followers. By the way, He is still doing that today—calling disciples. He is looking for followers, not fans.

Read the passage and see if you can pick out the philosophy of iniquity, the singular fundamental commitment that creates fans of Jesus, but not followers:

> *"And it came to pass, that, as they went in the way,*
> *a certain man said unto him, Lord,*
> *I will follow thee whithersoever thou goest.*
>
> *And Jesus said unto him, Foxes have holes,*
> *and birds of the air have nests;*
> *but the Son of man hath not where to lay his head.*
>
> *And he said unto another, Follow me.*
> *But he said, Lord,*
> *suffer me first to go and bury my father.*
>
> *Jesus said unto him, Let the dead bury their dead:*
> *but go thou and preach the kingdom of God.*
>
> *And another also said, Lord, I will follow thee;*
> *but let me first go bid them farewell,*
> *which are at home at my house.*
>
> *And Jesus said unto him,*
> *No man, having put his hand to the plough,*
> *and looking back, is fit for the kingdom of God."*
> (Luke 9:57-62)

Read it again if you have to. The philosophy of iniquity is stated two times by three different prospective disciples. I'm almost certain you identified it. The philosophy of iniquity stated in this passage is, "Let *me first.*" That's it! *"Me first!"*

Notice that these three prospects were real prospects. They were interested in Jesus. They were probably sincere, in that after their "me first" issue, they wouldn't mind fitting some discipleship into their busy lives. My friend, millions today are fans of Jesus. They don't mind fitting Jesus in somewhere, as long as it's not too inconvenient. "I'll see you in the church service on Sunday." But if they are up too late the night before, or company comes, or there is a football game, or there are errands to run, or there is inclement weather, or I just needed some alone time, or I got a phone call, or there was a special television program, or a family member needed me, or I got a job opportunity, and the excuses go on and on and on, *ad infinitum.*

American Christendom became quite popular when it didn't require us to give up much of anything. It was marketed to us. With the Santa Clause approach we were assured that we could be "Christian" by receiving "Santa's" gifts and still continue our "me first" philosophy. And we have. And now look where it has brought us. Our "me first" philosophy has us thinking that far beyond not being merely inconvenienced, we can be or do any vile thing and still be on our way to heaven.

Christendom is in this condition because we have not understood the devastations of iniquity nor how to eliminate past iniquities, conquer present iniquity, and prevent future iniquity. We have been taught false gospels.

Iniquity doesn't merely cause the gross, socially unacceptable sins (a severe tragedy of our day is that almost all gross sins have now become socially acceptable in this culture). Iniquity causes a soft disposition towards all sin; it will even redefine it into *not sin.* The PC (politically correct) liar now says he just "misspoke." In the following verses, when referring to this condition, God uses the term *woe*, which means "Oh-oh! Big trouble."

*"Woe unto them that draw **iniquity**
with cords of vanity,
and sin as it were with a cart rope."*
(Isaiah 5:18)

Two verses later, that iniquity is defined, and again the preface is, *"Woe."*

*"Woe unto them that call evil good, and good evil;
that put darkness for light, and light for darkness;
that put bitter for sweet, and sweet for bitter!*

*Woe unto them that are wise in their own eyes,
and prudent in their own sight!*

*Woe unto them that are mighty to drink wine,
and men of strength to mingle strong drink:*

*Which justify the wicked for reward,
and take away the righteousness
of the righteous from him!"*
(Isaiah 5:20-23)

This is another Bible list of the consequences of iniquity. It causes the reinterpretation of evil. It says it's really okay when it's not. It says that evil is good. Our culture celebrates behaviors of which we should be ashamed. Iniquity causes the mocking and downplaying of good. And it causes its victims to be "*right and prudent in their own eyes*" when, in fact, they are not. There's not much "*blushing*" anymore:

*"Were they ashamed when they
had committed abomination?
nay, they were not at all ashamed,
neither could they blush:
therefore they shall fall among them that fall:
at the time that I visit them
they shall be cast down, saith the LORD.*

*Thus saith the LORD,*
*Stand ye in the ways, and see,*
*and ask for the old paths,*
*where is the good way, and walk therein,*
*and ye shall find rest for your souls.*
*But they said, We will not walk therein."*
(Jeremiah 6:15-16)

*"Abomination"* means *morally disgusting.* But instead of disgust and outrage—no shame, no blushing! Then the Scriptures tell us to stand still, take a look around, and call for the *"old paths."* But that's old fashioned. Yep! But it's the good way. And if we walk in it, we will have mental health, emotional strength, and social stability. Iniquity causes the redefining of immorality as morality.

But it gets worse. Iniquity is a fundamental motive, an ultimate intention for why we do things. Thus it contaminates even good works.

So now we are beginning to see clearly that (1) Iniquity is the energizer behind sin; (2) Iniquity causes persons to redefine evil and call evil *good* and good *evil*; (3) Iniquity also contaminates good things because of its wicked, selfish motive.

Perhaps this understanding of the consequences of iniquity will help us give attention to our gross spiritual condition.

The following is a partial list of what selfishness and iniquity produces in our lives:

1. Makes decisions only on the basis of perceived personal advantage.

2. Denies Divine access to our lives because of the contest of wills.

3. Causes disregard for the well-being of others, except as we are able to benefit from them in some way.

4. Destroys wisdom, the ability to respond to life situations from God's point of view.

5. Creates the bondage of self-tyranny. We become our own slave-drivers.

6. Opposes genuine love.

7. Prevents proper self-love.

8. Causes over-indulgences of food, accumulation of stuff, entertainments, etc.

9. Perceives moral standards as blocks to happiness.

10. Creates unsustainability and often debt, because selfishness is insatiable.

11. Usurps the proper place of God in our lives: the "God Position" is taken over by the exalted ego.

12. Disregards the development of character qualities unless they are perceived to create self-advantage (e.g. "honesty is the best policy").

13. Creates a common bond with Satan, for at the core, he has the same philosophy.

14. Makes us "users" of others.

15. Eliminates the genuineness of love and friendship.

16. Creates conflicts with the selfishness of others.

17. Gives others no option but compliance to our demands or expectations.

18. Leads to the judging of others.

19. Shrinks our world of influence.

20. Causes disrespect for authorities.

21. Perverts geniune prayer, because prayer is now perceived as getting our will done on earth through heaven.

22. Prevents the heart from authentically saying to God, "Thy will be done."

23. Creates the inability to suffer when it is proper to do so.

24. Eliminates martyrdom.

25. Produces counterfeit Christianity.

26. Accommodates being religious, but is in essence self-rulership instead of Christ-rulership.

27. Causes misspending and/or over-spending and/or debt.

28. Causes inflated ideas of our own importance.

29. Blinds us to recognizing our own sins.

30. Causes us to think ourselves smarter than everyone else.

31. Artificially elevates our ideas above the ideas and thoughts of God and His Word.

32. Makes us think we don't need anyone else; independence from community.

33. Denies realities and lives in a fantasy world of self-exalting day-dreams.

34. Causes projection, attributing to others what we find unaccept-able in ourselves.

35. Provokes rationalization, making excuses for our behaviors

36. Makes us lie to protect ourselves.

37. Makes us hypocrites, presenting a false image to others.

38. Results in living for happiness rather than usefulness.

39. Causes us to judge others by their actions, while judging our-selves by our intentions.

40. Makes us break speed limits and run red lights.

41. Attempts to constantly control others, refusing to accept the "no" or the boundaries set by others.

42. Creates an inability to admit when we are wrong.

43. Produces the need for constant approval of others.

44. Makes our needs more important than the needs of others.

45. Causes quarreling to get our own way.

46. Produces jealousy at the success of others.

47. Produces laziness.

48. Causes an "I owe it to myself" attitude.

49. Corrupts good manners, except where such manners help our image.

50. Makes us manipulators of people and circumstances to achieve our own agenda.

51. Causes us to live for nothing bigger than ourselves.

52. Provokes us to do good works merely to make ourselves feel good.

53. Causes ungratefulness, which is not expressing appreciation for benefits (although the more refined iniquity is, the more it learns to express gratefulness; because perhaps in doing so, it will invoke more benefits).

## Chapter Nine

# The Benefits
# of
# Conquering Iniquity

*"Unto you first God,*
*having raised up his Son Jesus,*
*sent him to bless you, in turning away*
*every one of you from his iniquities."*
(Acts 3:26)

The will of God for your life is exactly what you would choose if you knew all the facts. Every direction we get from God is an indication of His love for us. Every instruction is for our betterment. And what is a command, but an instruction with urgency: an urgency that requires the knowledge of consequences. A command is a guideline to our success and/or a deterrent to our failure. Love does such things. Love blesses. Being turned away from our iniquities, is no exception.

*"Unto you first God,*
*having raised up his Son Jesus,*
*sent him to **bless you,***
***in turning away every one of you***
***from his iniquities."***
(Acts 3:26)

It is a severe understatement to say that getting rid of iniquity is a blessing. Iniquity is a damning condition that warrants eternal punishment and isolation from the kingdom of God. Being turned from our iniquities is the fundamental issue in basic salvation. However, there are many temporal, as well as eternal, benefits of conquering iniquity. Job and his friends were very aware of the benefits of conquering iniquity and listed them for us.

> *"If **iniquity** be in thine hand, put it far away,*
> *and let not wickedness dwell in thy tabernacles.*
> *For **then shalt thou** . . ."*
> (Job 11:14)

All of these listed benefits are found directly in this Scripture passage. They follow the *"for then"* of verse fourteen.

## 1. You will be able to look the world right in the eye.

> *"For then shalt thou lift up thy face without spot . . ."*
> (Job 11:15)

God does many remarkable things in our lives. One such work of God is the lifting up of our heads (see Psalm 3:3). Others can lift up our hands (see Hebrews 12:12) but only God can lift our heads. He delivers us from shame and, as in this passage, the shame of our past iniquities. So keep your chin up (but not your nose).

## 2. You will have stability.

> *". . . yea, thou shalt be stedfast . . ."*
> (Job 11:15)

Iniquity drives us in many directions, and often at the same time. James tells us that *"A double minded man is unstable in all his ways"* (James 1:8). It is iniquity that creates instability, because man was never intended to direct his own ways. It is not in man to do so:

*"O LORD, I know that the way of man is not in himself:*
*it is not in man that walketh to direct his steps."*
(Jeremiah 10:23)

## 3. You will live without fear.

*". . . yea, thou shalt be stedfast, and shalt not fear."*
(Job 11:15)

In this passage we learn that fear comes from the uncertainty and fickleness of iniquity. Scripture tells us that *". . . fear hath torment"* (1 John 4:18). The important question, however, is from whence cometh this fear? We know that fear does not come from God: *"For God hath not given us the spirit of fear; but of power, and of love, and of a sound mind"* (2 Timothy 1:7). When an unqualified driver is behind the wheel, every thinking person on board will experience fear because the wrong person is in control. Remember, sin is a matter of wrong conduct, but iniquity is a matter of wrong relationship. The wrong person is steering.

## 4. You will recover from the past.

*"Because thou shalt forget thy misery,*
*and remember it as waters that pass away."*
(Job 11:16)

The termination of iniquity qualifies God, as we shall soon see, to remove all past iniquities, as well as sins. God does not pardon what He does not  prevent. The dynamics of the full salvation process include such deliverance from the past that sin and iniquity are not only forgiven but cleansed; not only cleansed but remitted; and in the remission is the inability of the past to continue damaging the present or the future. It is now "water under the bridge," or as the Scriptures say it, *"as waters that pass away."*

## 5. You will feel younger.

*"And thine age shall be clearer than the noonday . . ."*
(Job 11:17)

Iniquity is a hard taskmaster. The ruling self is a cruel tyrant: ". . . the way of the transgressors is hard" (Proverbs 13:15). The unsurrendered ego drives; it doesn't lead. Once iniquity is purged, the tyrant is removed. Living is no longer like having sand in the gears. Energy, life, and youthfulness are renewed. God is not a hard taskmaster. This was the mistake made by the servant in the parable of the talents. He said, *"Lord, I knew thee that thou art an hard man"* (Matthew 25:24). He was wrong about that—dead wrong. A wrong concept about God leads to a wrong relationship with God. And a wrong relationship with God leads to wrong conduct, and wrong conduct is destructive. Conquering iniquity leads to a renewable youthfulness. David gives us clear supporting affirmation in this passage, that when our iniquities are forgiven, our youth is renewed like the eagle's: *"Who forgiveth all thine iniquities; who healeth all thy diseases; Who redeemeth thy life from destruction; who crowneth thee with lovingkindness and tender mercies; Who satisfieth thy mouth with good things; so that thy youth is renewed like the eagle's* (Psalms 103:3-5). An interesting study of Scripture would be to discover the other factors that renew our youthfulness.

**6. You will have influence.**

*". . . thou shalt shine forth . . ."*
(Job 11:17)

Whenever Scripture refers to our light shining or not shining, it is referring to our ability to influence. This is the plain meaning of Jesus when He said, *"Ye are the light of the world. A city that is set on an hill cannot be hid. Neither do men light a candle, and put it under a bushel, but on a candlestick; and it giveth light unto all that are in the house. Let your light so shine before men, that they may see your good works, and glorify your Father which is in heaven"* (Matthew 5:14-16). This is having influence.

In contrast with this we have learned, *"Whoso curseth his father or his mother, his lamp shall be put out in obscure darkness"* (Proverbs 20:20). Such a person shall lose his ability to properly influence others.

## 7. You will be refreshed.

> *". . . thou shalt be as the morning."*
> (Job 11:17)

Morning is often used poetically in Scripture to represent the reality of newness or refreshing. For example, the mercies and compassions of the Lord toward us are new every morning: "*It is of the LORD'S mercies that we are not consumed, because his compassions fail not. They are new every morning: great is thy faithfulness*" (Lamentations 3:22-23). There are a number of sources of refreshing in Scripture. Each of them should be discovered by us. The passage that we are considering here is quite plain: the removal of iniquity will create this refreshing—this renewing—just like a morning.

## 8. You will be secure.

> *"And thou shalt be secure . . ."*
> (Job 11:18)

You are now in the hands of God, an artist who makes no blunders and no mistakes—none whatsoever. From self-rule to Christ's rule! The government of your life is now upon His shoulders: "*For unto us a child is born, unto us a son is given: and the government shall be upon his shoulder: and his name shall be called Wonderful, Counsellor, The mighty God, The everlasting Father, The Prince of Peace*" (Isaiah 9:6). He is up to the task. He is strong enough. But His real right to rule is founded in His love and wisdom. You can trust Him. You will be secure forever. Keep your life in His hand. No one else can take you away from Him and your security in Him:

*"And I give unto them eternal life; and they shall never perish, neither shall any man pluck them out of my hand. My Father, which gave them me, is greater than all; and no man is able to pluck them out of my Father's hand"* (John 10:28-29).

## 9. You will be optimistic.

> *". . . because there is hope . . ."*
> (Job 11:18)

The transfer from a life of iniquity to a life under the rule of God—the created under The Creator—brings with it an unequaled optimism. The popular psychological systems of our day (e.g. Freud, Skinner, and Jung) try to get us to believe that our future is determined by our past. According to them, the reason you behave the way you do today is because of the things that happened in your childhood.

Jesus, on the other hand, seemed to reject the limitations of cultural or environmental determinism. He indicated that we act the way we do today because of the future, not the past: *"For we are saved by hope: but hope that is seen is not hope: for what a man seeth, why doth he yet hope for? But if we hope for that we see not, then do we with patience wait for it"* (Romans 8:24-25). We are controlled, not by our past, but by our future: by what we hope. We study today because we hope to graduate later. We practice the piano today because we will give a recital in three months' time.

Deliverance from iniquity takes away bondages and frees us. We now have a hope, a fresh optimism, because the God that is now properly enthroned in the leadership and management position of our lives has great plans for the future: *"For I know the thoughts that I think toward you, saith the LORD, thoughts of peace, and not of evil, to give you an expected end"* (Jeremiah 29:11).

## 10. You will be safe.

> *". . . yea, thou shalt dig about thee,*
> *and thou shalt take thy rest in safety."*
> (Job 11:18)

Did you know that, *". . . safety is of the Lord"* (Proverbs 21:31)? God is interested in both your eternal and temporal safety. He is looking out for you! Every benefit of becoming iniquity-free makes the steps to freedom from iniquity worthwhile. Safety and rest are no exception.

## 11. You will sleep without fear.

> *"Also thou shalt lie down,*
> *and none shall make thee afraid . . ."*
> (Job 11:19)

You will *"not be afraid for the terror by night . . ."* (Psalm 91:5). Being free of iniquity will give you what David had when he said, *"I will both lay me down in peace, and sleep: for thou, LORD, only makest me dwell in safety"* (Psalm 4:8). Peace is the opposite of fear.

## 12. Many will come to you for counsel and help.

> *". . . yea, many shall make suit unto thee."*
> (Job 11:19)

People do not seek guidance and help from iniquitous persons. Why? Because a person motivated by iniquity has a conflict of interest—a wrong motive—be it financial profit or some other personal advantage. The adequate solution to iniquity frees us from all ulterior motives. When others discern this pureness in us they will seek counsel.

Others will be able to testify, *"Concerning the works of men, by the word of thy lips I have kept me from the paths of the destroyer"* (Psalm 17:4).

Then the passage in Job concludes with a warning to those who do not put away iniquity:

> *"But the eyes of the wicked shall fail,*
> *and they shall not escape,*
> *and their hope shall be*
> *as the giving up of the ghost."*
> (Job 11:20)

We now move to another passage of Job where additional benefits are listed. Take special note that the benefits are the direct result of putting away iniquity.

*"If thou return to the Almighty,*
*thou shalt be built up,*
***thou shalt put away iniquity***
*far from thy tabernacles.*

*Then shalt thou . . ."*
(Job 22:23-24)

## 13. You will be able to save money.

*"Then shalt thou lay up gold as dust,*
*and the gold of Ophir*
*as the stones of the brooks."*
(Job 22:24)

Iniquity wastes money. It drives you to shop. It justifies spending more than you earn. It is the cause of debt. Iniquity recognizes no financial principle that, in its short-sighted way of seeing, does not contribute to its immediate self-gratification.

On the other hand, when God is directing our affairs we will have savings, and money to spare: *". . . It is He that giveth thee power to get wealth . . ."* (Deuteronomy 8:18). While iniquity can cause riches, the riches come with a multitude of negative factors that actually leave you a poor person with money. Real blessing is riches without sorrows: *"The blessing of the LORD, it maketh rich, and he addeth no sorrow with it"* (Proverbs 10:22). It may be unusual for an author to advertise in the middle of his writing, but I have written another book describing the iniquity free-way to riches. It's called *God's Way To Riches.*

## 14. God Himself will watch out for you and provide for you.

*"Yea, the Almighty shall be thy defence,*
*and thou shalt have plenty of silver."*
(Job 22:25)

Leaving iniquity behind brings you into a kingdom, a relationship where God Himself assumes responsibility for your well-being. His care includes refuge, fortress, defense, deliverance, protection, shielding, early warnings, foresight, clear vision, and a host of other benefits. Perhaps these truths are what inspired Doctor Charles J. Rolls—who was named after the Honorable Charles Rolls, and joined with Frederick H. Royce in 1906, to found the Rolls-Royce Company—to write in his masterful way:

The fountain of His fullness never fails.
The reservoir of His resources never recede
The wisdom of his Word never wains.
The vigor of His virtue never varies.
The burnish of His beauty never blemishes.
The luster of His love never lessens.
The power of His prowess never perishes.

(The World's Greatest Name IV, C.J. Rolls ©1956, Zondervan Publishing House)

How *"unsearchable the riches of Christ"* (Ephesians 3:8)! They are unsearchable not because they cannot be found, but because they are inexhaustible. Surely such was the concern and passion of Jeremiah when he proclaimed, *"Your **iniquities** have turned away these things, and your sins have withholden good things from you"* (Jeremiah 5:25). God will be your defense, and you will have plenty!

## 15. Your delight will be in the Lord.

*"For then shalt thou have thy delight in the Almighty . . ."*
(Job 22:26)

What delights you? Do you not find it amazing that people take delight in trivialities? We chase after trinkets and tinsel and call it a delight. This is the query of Paul: *"Howbeit then, when ye knew not God, ye did service unto them which by nature are no gods. But now, after that ye have known God, or rather are known of God, how turn ye again to the weak and beggarly elements, whereunto ye desire again to be in bondage?"* (Galatians 4:8-9).

I suggest to you that this is the work of iniquity: chasing after gods that are no gods. The Scriptures affirm this surely. Look at the contrast between our delights and those of the iniquitous. To us the thoughts of God are our delight, because we have real and sweet fellowship with the Lord. But can those with iniquity on the throne have any fellowship with God or enjoy Him? Let the Scriptures answer:

> *"In the multitude of my thoughts within me*
> *thy comforts delight my soul.*
>
> *Shall the **throne of iniquity** have fellowship with thee,*
> *which frameth mischief by a law?"*
> (Psalm 94:19-20)

Our delight is in the Lord! The poverty of the church's condition is best demonstrated by the lengths to which modern church leadership goes to attract to church—and keep attracted to church—those who have no delight in the Lord. How this contrasts to what David said:

> *"One thing have I desired of the LORD,*
> *that will I seek after;*
> *that I may dwell in the house of the LORD*
> *all the days of my life,*
> *to behold the beauty of the LORD,*
> *and to enquire in his temple."*
> (Psalm 27:4)

## 16. You will be looking to the Lord to meet your needs.

*". . . and shalt lift up thy face unto God."*
(Job 22:26)

Which way we're looking in times of need, discouragement, or loneliness indicates much about us. The source to whom we look demonstrates our true faith. Whoever or whatever we look to also receives our reverence, allegiance, affections, and devotion. The apostle Paul affirms that it is *"My God"* that *"shall supply all your need according to his riches in glory by Christ Jesus"* (Philippians 4:19). The termination of iniquity also terminates looking unto any and every other replacement of God.

## 17. Your prayers shall be heard by God.

*"Thou shalt make thy prayer unto him,*
*and he shall hear thee . . .*
(Job 22:27)

What a delightful benefit, yea, how necessary! Prayer is one of the aspects most negatively impacted by iniquity. It is not an issue of whether iniquity prevents answers to prayer, but rather that iniquity prevents prayers from even being heard to begin with:

*"If I regard **iniquity** in my heart,*
*the Lord will not hear me."*
(Psalm 66:18)

It should not concern us today that a lot of prayers are not answered or not even heard. Prayer has been perverted into getting my will done on earth through heaven, instead of having to do with getting His will done on earth through me. Imagine what a crime we embark upon when we try to get God—the God of the whole universe, with all His wisdom and power—to become the servant of our wills, the servant of our iniquities, the slave of our selfishness. That is what much praying has become: a twisting of God's arm to get Him to do what we want done.

It has been taught that if we could get enough people saying the same thing to God enough times we would somehow be able to persuade Him to do what He appears reluctant to do. David gives us the key and then goes on to testify further. Let's read this whole joyful context:

*"Come and hear, all ye that fear God,*
*and I will declare what he hath done for my soul.*

*I cried unto him with my mouth,*
*and he was extolled with my tongue.*

*If I regard **iniquity** in my heart,*
*the Lord will not hear me:*

*But verily God hath heard me;*
*he hath attended to the voice of my prayer.*

*Blessed be God,*
*which hath not turned away my prayer,*

*nor his mercy from me."*
(Psalm 66:16-20)

The end of iniquity is the beginning of genuine prayer! Listen to James: *". . . The effectual fervent prayer of a righteous man availeth much"* (James 5:16). A righteous man is a *rightly-related-to-God* man. It is the prayers of a rightly-related-to-God man that are effective. Iniquity is a wrong relationship, an out-of-right relationship, with God.

Yet iniquity causes something far worse than our prayers not being heard by God:

*"Behold, the LORD'S hand is not shortened,*
*that it cannot save;*
*neither his ear heavy, that it cannot hear:*

> *But your iniquities have separated*
> *between you and your God,*
> *and your sins have hid his face from you,*
> *that he will not hear."*
> (Isaiah 59:1-2)

It is terrible and tragic enough that iniquity prevents our prayers from being heard, but this verse indicates something much more devastating than that. What could be worse? It is iniquity that causes us to be separated from God! And so great is that separation that we are out of hearing distance.

I once read a bumper sticker on a car which said, "If God seems far away, guess who moved." We have! But wherein have we separated ourselves from God? By iniquity!

So here we learn that one of the very great benefits of terminating iniquity is that our prayers will get a hearing with God. Of greater importance, however, is that we will no longer be separated from the presence of God! Let us be careful not to conjure up artificial feelings of the presence of God. There's a big difference between mood music and the real presence of God.

## 18. You will have the ability to keep your word.

> *". . . and thou shalt pay thy vows."*
> (Job 22:27)

Iniquity is at the root of a man's unwillingness or inability to keep his word. It is the cause of broken vows, broken promises, lying, deceit, and unfulfilled commitments. It is an iniquity to be unequal to the truth or unequal to our word given. Iniqui*ties*, as well as sins, are the natural overflow from *Iniquity*, the condition of the heart.

When the "I" is enthroned in the place reserved for God only, it rules by its whims and values. Consequently, keeping vows and keeping one's word becomes more a matter of convenience, or relevant only when keeping our word is perceived as serving our own interests.

On the other hand, when God is enthroned in His rightful place in our lives, iniquity is terminated and we live by His precepts. This causes all behaviors, including the keeping of our word, to be controlled by principle-based convictions. This change at the ownership-level (the heart) affects all executive decisions thereafter. This is reflected in the ability to keep our words and promises, as well as our zeal to do so—regardless of cost or inconvenience.

*"That which is gone out of thy lips*
*thou shalt keep and perform;"*
(Deuteronomy 23:23)

*". . . He that sweareth to his own hurt, and changeth not"* (Psalm 15:4) is one of the evidences listed for those who really are in relationship with God. The passage concludes with the staggering proclamation, *"He that doeth these things shall never be moved"* (Psalm 15:5).

The Scriptures declare that the man who does not keep his vows is a fool, *"When thou vowest a vow unto God, defer not to pay it; for he hath no pleasure in fools . . ."* (Ecclesiastes 5:4). We could understand it easier if the Scriptures called the vow-breaker a liar, or better yet, a terrible liar, because he attached a vow to his word. But how are we to understand that God calls this person a fool? I suggest that it is because God does not rule in the fool's heart; iniquity does! For, *"The fool hath said in his heart, There is no God"* (Psalm 53:1).

The fool hath said in his heart, "there is no God in my heart except me." To verify this is iniquity, we must read it in the context. Let's see it all together: *"The fool hath said in his heart, There is no God. Corrupt are they, and have done abominable iniquity . . ."* (Psalm 53:1).

When iniquity is terminated, the foolishness of the fool is terminated. When a man ceases to be a fool he keeps his word all the time, every time. It is the termination of iniquity that enables, empowers, and inspires a person to keep his word.

## 19. You will have the proper ability of self-determination.

*"Thou shalt also decree a thing,*
*and it shall be established unto thee . . ."*
(Job 22:28)

Iniquity is the perversion of the legitimate and proper ability of self-determination. Iniquity thrives on self-determination. In fact, absolute unfettered self-determination would be a good definition of iniquity. Iniquity is intent on doing one's own will, so much so that it is willing, able, and zealous to usurp the role of any and every authority, including God's. It is the unfettered, uncontrolled, and unsubmitted-to-proper-authority will of man that makes him a god-player. He has taken over the rightful place of God.

In His usual way of making everything plain, Jesus said, *"If any man will come after me, let him deny himself, and take up his cross, and follow me"* (Matthew 16:24). Denying self, as we shall see more clearly in later chapters, is denying self of taking over God's role. Christ's terms are clear.

The will of God is to be ultimate in the life of every true follower. Nothing we say, do, or intend can be contrary to the will of God. If we determine to say, do, or intend contrary to God, we evidence that we have taken over the God position. We are still in iniquity. We are playing god. Everything we will, as true followers, should be subject to His will. We are to pray, *". . . Thy will be done in earth, as it is in heaven"* (Matthew 6:10). The *"in earth"* includes *in me, in my life.*

This is a critical issue to all praying: *"And this is the confidence that we have in him, that, if we ask any thing according to his will, he heareth us: And if we know that he hear us, whatsoever we ask, we know that we have the petitions that we desired of him"* (1 John 5:14-15).

All true Christians determine to do His will: first, foremost, and always. There is no competition and no contest of wills anymore. We settled that at the ownership-level and every executive decision—a decision to execute or bring into reality—is now based on carrying out the original intent, the will of God. Our will is subservient to God's all the time, every time.

However, when the iniquity issue is resolved—God is enthroned and God's will is being done—He still leaves us a sphere of self-determination. It is a jurisdiction with parameters, scope, and dimension. It is not absolute. It is limited and contained and still subject to His approval and/or adjustment. Within this sphere we are given a latitude of self-determination that is proper, legitimate, and affirmed in this text: *"Thou shalt also decree a thing, and it shall be established unto thee . . ."* (Job 22:28).

## 20. You will be able to see where you are going in life.

*". . . and the light shall shine upon thy ways."*
(Job 22:28)

Most people do not know where they are going. They are being rushed across the stage of time with little or no comprehension of where or why or what is at stake. When they get to the exit sign they suspect there must have been something they should have done or something they should have been. But they know not what! Very few know why the world began, why they are here, where they are going, or what the main issues of life are about. This blindness is caused by iniquity. Iniquity separates us from the only one who knows the answers to these questions—someone outside ourselves, someone with a larger perspective, the one in charge of the big picture—God! Jeremiah testified to it: *"O LORD, I know that the way of man is not in himself: it is not in man that walketh to direct his steps"* (Jeremiah 10:23).

Solomon penned it this way, *"Man's goings are of the LORD; how can a man then understand his own way?"* (Proverbs 20:24).

This is the paramount question: how can a man understand his own way? Everyone becomes a philosopher to some degree or another. Unfortunately, we end up with a lot of *foolosophy*: minds that fail to find the answers to these burning questions and are willing to settle for notions, absurdities, and the ridiculous and then to spend the rest of their lives banking on these figments of imagination and lying vanities.

It is not in man to understand. He must find the answers outside of himself. The only one beyond us that is qualified to answer is the Creator. What a novel idea for many. Perhaps the Creator knows why we're here, and where we should be going and what are the main issues!

This is why we are warned so forcefully, *"Beware lest any man spoil you through philosophy and vain deceit, after the tradition of men, after the rudiments of the world, and not after Christ"* (Colossians 2:8). And again, *"But avoid foolish questions, and genealogies, and contentions, and strivings about the law; for they are unprofitable and vain"* (Titus 3:9).

Paul passionately wrote fatherly advice to young Timothy, his son in the faith and a pastor at a young but mature age: *"O Timothy, keep that which is committed to thy trust, avoiding profane and vain babblings, and oppositions of science falsely so called: Which some professing have erred concerning the faith"* (1 Timothy 6:20-21).

Note the phrase *"oppositions of science falsely so called."* These days are dangerous. They are perilous: *"This know also, that in the last days perilous times shall come"* (2 Timothy 3:1). Misguidance is proliferated and even celebrated. Distortion abounds. Science has become a joke. Imagine with me for a moment the mentality of someone who looks at a simple pen, a writing instrument, and says,

"There is no pen maker!" To look at creation and say, "There is no Creator!" is the zenith of arrogance and iniquity.

However gross these stupidities are, they are not the product of a mere lack of knowledge, logic, or dialectics. They are the deliberate choices of men who have committed the ultimate act of intellectual suicide and treason to deny the Creator: to deny God. A mind that is thus warped will stop at no lengths to establish his own ways, his own agenda, and his own kingdom where he sits as god. This is iniquity. As he continues to play god he can pursue his immoral ways, unhindered by the being he denies, and yet who is very much there—watching, waiting, longing, and loving!

I long ago decided I would rather have a knowledge of the Bible without an education than to have an education without a knowledge of the Bible. Fortunately, most of us these days no longer have to choose between the two. However, if faced with this option, be sure to choose the Bible. That is how you will know where you are going.

It is not in man to know his way. It is in God, the Creator. Without iniquity, the light will shine on your ways and you will be able to say with David, *"Thy word is a lamp unto my feet, and a light unto my path"* (Psalm 119:105).

### 21. You will have a ministry of encouragement to others.

*When men are cast down,*
*then thou shalt say, There is lifting up . . ."*
(Job 22:29)

There are two kinds of *"lifting up."* One is by self-promotion and the other by God. Both are set forth in this Scripture: *"And whosoever shall exalt himself shall be abased; and he that shall humble himself shall be exalted"* (Matthew 23:12).

Iniquity is the exalting of self: making myself unequal to what I was designed by God to be, or do, at a given time in life. The self-help books that line our stores most frequently appeal to our iniquity, to our self-promotion schemes: getting ahead, winning, pulling our own strings, getting what we want, out-performing the competition, out-smarting the resistance, climbing the ladder, striving for the top.

So we learn the techniques, the tricks, the politics, the principles of selling and manipulation. With varying degrees of what we perceive to be success, we strive onward in our quest for whatever we think is ultimate for us. No success is really gratifying, because iniquity can never be satisfied. The insatiable appetite for *the ultimate* would require a person to exchange places with God. Sound familiar?

First of all, such ascendancy is impossible. Neither you nor I will ever be God. If we ever were, we wouldn't know what to do. And can you imagine the devastation we would bring to the entire universe if we had god-powers to carry out our selfishness in unrestricted measure? Iniquity creates self-centeredness. When we conquer iniquity, we will be able to view others in a caring way. That will produce a ministry of encouragement.

## 22. Those that are humble will be saved by your message.

*". . . and he shall save the humble person."*
(Job 22:29)

Oh the blessing of our being able to help others—to heal, to rescue, to save. It is true that not everyone will receive the help we offer. There are two major factors which determine whether or not others can be helped. First, the prideful versus humble condition of those you would desire to help. It takes humility to be the student and not the teacher, the learner and not the instructor. Many cannot receive help because of their pride.

The second factor which determines whether or not others can be helped, (and the one we can control), is the character and qualifications of ourselves, the helpers. This is determined by our character, whether or not we are helping for iniquitous reasons. Being without iniquity means we have no personal agenda, no hidden motives, no conflict of interest, and no built-in self-benefits. The iniquity-free person is the only one who can have genuine (and I mean *genuine*) love. For what is love, but the choosing of the highest good of another without personal profit as a motive? Iniquity always has an agenda of its own: its own exaltation or self-interest.

If you conquer iniquity, you will be able to save others.

### 23. Deliverance will come to those separated from evil.

*"He shall deliver the island of the innocent . . ."*
(Job 22:30)

Often the main reason those we try to help will not receive godly or righteous instruction from us, is that they don't see us as being any better or any different than themselves. Iniquity is easy to detect. And while we may appear caring in reaching out our helping hands, most people are suspicious. Your ability to deliver others is postulated upon being iniquity-free. Remember how this text began: *"If iniquity be in thine hand, put it far away, and let not wickedness dwell in thy tabernacles. For then shalt thou . . ."* (Job 11:14). If they can be helped, if they can be saved, if they can be delivered, if they are innocent (meaning *free of suspicion of us*), they can and will be delivered. But there is one more aspect of being iniquity-free that affects others.

### 24. Their deliverance is related to pureness of your iniquity-free condition.

*". . . and it is delivered by the pureness of thine hands."*
(Job 22:30)

A little iniquity will poison the whole process. A cherry pie may only have a little poison in it. In the Scriptural illustration, a little leaven leavens the whole:

*"Your glorying is not good.*
*Know ye not that a little leaven*
*leaveneth the whole lump?*


*Purge out therefore the old leaven,*
*that ye may be a new lump, as ye are unleavened . . ."*
(1 Corinthians 5:6-7)

In essence, pureness—the absence of any mixture—is essential. No hidden motives, no personal agenda, no conflict of interest, no iniquity; just the cleanness of our hands and the pureness of our motives.

# CHAPTER TEN

# How The Gospel Resolves Iniquity

*"He will turn again,*
*He will have compassion upon us;*
*He will subdue our iniquities . . ."*
(Micah 7:19)

If we are wrong about the gospel, we are wrong about everything. The stakes are highest on this fundamental. It appears that the gospel in modern American Christianity has been reduced to a sloppy, slothful, slanderous aberration. Where is the supernatural? You know the one I mean. The gospel that is *"the power of God unto salvation to everyone that believeth"* (Romans 1:16). Where is the gospel that makes *"old things pass away and all things become new"* (2 Corinthians 5:17)? The industrialization of Christianity has brought entirely too many compromises; some of them have far-reaching devastations.

The present gospel being preached or marketed is a gospel of forgiveness only, presuming justification without any sanctifying powers. Does this gospel, in fact, save *from* sin or does it "save" *in* sin. Does the gospel have the power to save from sinning or does it not? Which gospel do you believe? Are we really transformed and translated from the kingdom of darkness to the kingdom of light, and from the kingdom of Satan to the kingdom of God?

We know what kingdom we are in, by who our king is. We get into a kingdom by swearing allegiance to a king. I tell people somewhat humorously, but factually (and certainly joyfully), that I was a Canadian by birth and became American by the grace of God; and I'm a southerner by choice. In fact, I like the bumper sticker that says, "I wasn't born in the south, but I got here as fast as I could." To become a citizen of America I had to pledge "Allegiance to the flag of the United States of America and to the Republic for which it stands, one nation under God, indivisible, with Liberty and Justice for all." Citizenship also requires the renunciation of allegiances to foreign nations.

Satan, once a good guy, once an archangel equal with Gabriel and Michael, became guilty of self-enthronement and lost the Kingdom of God. His iniquity, his self-enthronement, cost him everything. True conversion requires the termination of self-rule, which in its essence, is iniquity. Death to self-rule is the clear meaning of this oft cited Scripture:

> *"I am crucified with Christ: nevertheless I live;*
> *yet not I, but Christ liveth in me . . ."*
> (Galatians 2:20)

This is not the extermination of the self but the termination of self usurpation of God's rightful place. It is the crucifying of the self out of the god-position: the rulership and management position in our lives that should be reserved for only God Himself. The dethronement of self is surely the meaning in the immersion of water baptism: *"Therefore we are buried with Him by baptism into death . . ."* (Romans 6:4).

But as in baptism, this death, this burial that is symbolic of the termination of self-rule which must be true in our lives, is only half the story. It gets better. Baptism includes coming back up out of the water, back up out of the death-to-self-rule, to live the resurrected life. And what is that? It is the beginning of living life as it was designed for mankind by the Creator in the beginning: *". . . that like as Christ was raised up from the dead by the glory of the Father, even so we also should walk in newness of life"* (Romans 6:4). We are now to live a new life, an abundant life, a resurrected life, a life where Jesus Christ now occupies His rightful God-position in our lives. It is a life under His management, His lordship, His guidance.

Jesus has many names in the Bible. Here are a few: Jesus, Savior, Master, King, Counsellor, Wonderful, Rose of Sharon, Lily of the Valley, Bright and Morning Star, Fairest of Ten Thousand, Ancient of Days, Teacher, The Anointed One, Alpha and Omega, The Bread of Life, The Chief Cornerstone, The Lamb of God, Emmanuel, The Messiah, The Great Shepherd and many, many more.

But He has a name that is above all names. Jesus is *Lord*:

*". . . a name which is above every name:*

*That at the name of Jesus every knee should bow, of things in heaven, and things in earth, and things under the earth;*

*And that **every tongue should confess that Jesus Christ is Lord**, to the glory of God the Father."*
(Philippians 2:9-11)

In the Bible, the name *Savior* appears thirty-seven times. The name *Lord* is used 7,738 times. How could we have missed this?

The "No Lordship Gospel" has ushered us into an era of fake Christianity in the church where Jesus is not Lord (except perhaps in theory). Yes, theologians admit that He is Lord of the universe; but deny the necessity of His proper functioning position in each of our lives. The gospel has become a mere mental and academic assent to a short catechism of beliefs. Saving faith is not qualified, quantified, or evaluated. It is just assumed. Dietrich Bonnhoeffer had it straight when he said, "Only those who really believe, obey. And only those who obey, really believe." Unfortunately antinomianism is back in full strength and in vogue.

The truth is that the proper reception of a supernatural gospel will bring about a supernatural experience. And I do mean *proper reception*. The gospel requires a change of government, from self-rule to Christ-rule, from self-management to God's management. When Jesus Christ is received properly, that is to say, enthroned in our hearts unchallenged by ourselves, or anyone or anything, He—in that position of power—works miracles. As Lord and Master, He throws out the bad and the ugly and brings in the new and the beautiful. He cleanses past sins and iniquities (all of them) out of existence, out of existence, out of existence!

Never doubt that the God who created something out of nothing can also create nothing out of something. And that, my friend, is what He does with your sins. It's the new starting point of a new life with Jesus Christ properly enthroned in our hearts, in the management position, replacing the fake god (which was ourselves). You have heard it right, *"no man can serve two masters."* Let's look at the whole verse:

> *"No man can serve two masters:*
> *for either he will hate the one, and love the other;*
> *or else he will hold to the one, and despise the other.*
> *Ye cannot serve God and mammon."*
> (Matthew 6:24)

Caution! Caution! Make no mistake about the facts. There can be no competition; only one master can rule. It's either Him or me. Responding properly to what Christ has provided for us on His cross requires full surrender of the god-position in our lives to God Himself, and to no other—not peers, not culture, not friends, not religion, not even myself. The ego must be dethroned for Christ to be enthroned.

When that happens, the past is taken care of, including the past sins and the past iniquities. Look at the startling benefits:

*"Bless the LORD, O my soul,*
*and forget not all his benefits:*

*Who **forgiveth all thine iniquities;***
(Psalm 103:2-3)

Jesus intends to fix everything—everything! There is nothing broken that He can't fix. There's nothing lost that He can't recover. That is why we call Him Savior. That's why we call Him Redeemer. Rejoice with me! *"Let all that is within me bless His Holy name"* (Psalm 103:1).

With the past taken care of, Jesus now takes us forward from the present on into the future. We follow Him. Before, we wanted Him to follow us. But now He's the Lord (instead of me). What blessed relief! Now I am His to command. And I do mean, command. Once Jesus asked followers this question:

*"And why call ye me, Lord, Lord,*
*and do not the things which I say?"*
(Luke 6:46)

In essence, He was saying, "Why waste your breath. It is following that counts, not your feigned words, but obedience." Following is easy now that I have stopped playing god. Now He's the Leader. He's the Teacher, and I'm the student.

Is it easy? You bet! When we are properly yoked with Him. He said, *". . . my yoke is easy, and my burden is light"* (Matthew 11:29). It is so easy now. However, *". . . the way of transgressors is hard"* (Proverbs 13:15). Let's pause for a moment to see how easy it is:

*"Come unto me,*
*all ye that labour and are heavy laden,*
*and I will give you rest.*

127

*Take my yoke upon you, and learn of me;*
*for I am meek and lowly in heart:*
*and ye shall find rest unto your souls.*

*For my yoke is easy, and my burden is light."*
(Matthew 11:28-30)

1) Your labor ends.
2) Your load will be lighter.
3) You get refreshed.
4) You learn a new approach to life.
5) He is not a harsh leader but meek and lowly.
6) You will have mental health and emotional strength.
7) Your portion is light and easy.

What makes going forward easy? We just follow the leader. We discover the "Joy of Living By Commandment." Nothing He tells us, no instruction and no commandment, is irritating to us anymore. *"We keep his commandments: and his commandments are not grievous"* (1 John 5:3). His instructions and commands become happy guidelines to do that on which our hearts are now set. They used to irritate us. Why? Because they interfered with our iniquity, our previous agenda that was set by our nefarious god-playing.

Now we can say, *"I delight to do thy will, O my God: yea, thy law is within my heart"* (Psalm 40:8). Happy days are here! And what makes them so happy? We enjoy God. Reality has overcome my phony god acts. Now He reigns in me! For real!

What does it mean to have *The Joy of Living By Commandment*? Here it is:

"Before I decide, think, or act in any given situation,
I first enquire to see if God has a command that applies.
If so, I obey that command immediately,
joyfully, and without compromise."

That's it! Done! It's easy! And it's all I have to do the rest of my life. It's now settled. He rules. He is my God. There is no other. Any other authority that exists in my life must act within the parameters prescribed by the Lord God Himself, in His Word (this includes parents, teachers, employers, pastors, elders, and mentors). Only Jesus is Lord!

How does this affect future iniquity? The instructions and commands are severe instructions which have consequences attached to them to underscore their importance. They will always cause us to be motivated by love instead of iniquity. And those attitudes and actions, directed by God, have iniquity-prevention factors built into them. Follow Him and there will be zero iniquity.

The Scriptures speak the truth about us:

> *"All we like sheep have gone astray;*
> *we have turned every one to his own way;*
> *and the LORD hath laid on him the **iniquity** of us all."*
> (Isaiah 53:6)

We went astray. We turned, every one of us, to our own way; that is the essence of iniquity. But Jesus has taken care of it: *". . . the Lord hath laid on Him (Jesus), the iniquity of us all."*

# CHAPTER ELEVEN

# How To Recover From Past Iniquity

*"Bless the LORD, O my soul,*
*And forget not all his benefits:*

*Who forgiveth all thine iniquities;"*
(Psalm 103:2-3)

Recall that an adequate solution to iniquity requires that; 1) we recover from past iniquity; 2) we are able to terminate present iniquity; and 3) we prevent future iniquity. In this chapter we will learn how to recover from past iniquity.

Here's good news for you. You won't have much difficulty grasping this, for past iniquity is dealt with in much the same way as past sin. Why the similarity? It's because Jesus made provision for both on the cross. He bore both our sin and our iniquity. It should be of interest to us that the fifty-third chapter of Isaiah, where we are informed of this fact, goes on to give more details about iniquity:

*"He was wounded for our transgressions,*
*He was bruised for our iniquities . . .*

*. . . We have turned every one to his own way*
*And the Lord hath laid on Him the iniquity of us all.*

> *. . . By His knowledge shall my*
> *righteous servant justify many;*
> *for He shall bear their iniquities."*

**Past Iniquities Are Forgiven Out of Existence.**

Only God can do that. But it is not a trite act; it is an expensive one. Justice demands payment, and indeed, payment was made by our Dear Savior on the cross. It is true that our sins were laid upon Jesus. But it is equally true that our iniquities, yours and mine, were laid upon Him—separate and apart from our sins.

It should be noted that the same Scripture that reports that the *"Lord hath laid on Him the iniquity of us all,"* also includes an accurate definition of the essence of iniquity: *"we have turned every one to his own way."* Who can resist, at this point, declaring the great graciousness of our Savior; He took our sins and bore our iniquities— all of them, and for all of us. It is no wonder that Charles Wesley, one of the greatest hymn writers of all time, said he would have gladly given all of his hymns to have written the one authored by Isaac Watts in 1707. The music was written by Lowell Manson:

> When I survey the wondrous cross
> Upon which the Prince of Glory died,
> My richest gain I count but loss
> And pour contempt on all my pride.
>
> Forbid it, Lord, that I should boast,
> Save in the death of Christ my God!
> All the vain things that charm me most,
> I sacrifice them to His blood.
>
> See from His head, His hands, His feet,
> Sorrow and love flow mingled down!
> Did e'er such love and sorrow meet,
> Or thorns compose so rich a crown?

His dying crimson, like a robe,
Spreads o'er His body on the tree;
Then I am dead to all the globe,
And all the globe is dead to me.

Were the whole realm of nature mine,
That were a present far too small;
Love so amazing, so divine,
Demands my soul, my life, my all.

To Christ, who won for sinners grace
By bitter grief and anguish sore,
Be praise from all the ransomed race
Forever and forevermore.

We must never take forgiveness lightly. Its cost was immense and its benefits equally so. Let us be sure that forgiveness applies to iniquity as well as to sins:

*"Bless the Lord, O my soul,
and forget not all his benefits:*

*Who forgiveth all thine **iniquities** . . ."*
(Psalm 103:2-3)

Forgiveness of iniquities makes us indeed blessed, as Romans 4:7 affirms: *"Blessed are they whose iniquities are forgiven . . ."* Forgiveness is certainly amazing, glorious, and wonderful. A whole list of superlatives could be entered here. However, more than forgiveness is needed.

**Past Iniquities Are Cleansed.**

A bumper sticker says, "Christians Are Just Forgiven Sinners." NOT true! Forgiveness is essential, but inadequate. We must not be forgiven and still stuck with our iniquitous condition. We need to have iniquity cleaned out of us. We need a clean start. And Jesus provides that (this is a good time to say, "Hallelujah!" out loud).

*"And I will cleanse them from all their **iniquity**,*
*whereby they have sinned against me;*
*and I will pardon all their **iniquities**,*
*whereby they have sinned,*
*and whereby they have transgressed against me."*
(Jeremiah 33:8)

Jesus has provided a cleansing stream, a washing, healing stream. It is the red of Calvary. It's a stain remover that reaches where no other can. It reaches to the soul of a man or woman. It reaches where psychologists, psychiatrists, and counselors can never touch. Its results are manifested in a newness of life because the old is done away with, cleansed out of existence. You now get a clean slate, a new start. You can build anew:

*"In the day that I shall have*
***cleansed you from all your iniquities***
*I will also cause you to dwell in the cities,*
*and the wastes shall be builded.*

*And the desolate land shall be tilled,*
*whereas it lay desolate in the sight of all that passed by.*

*And they shall say,*
*This land that was desolate*
*is become like the garden of Eden . . ."*
(Ezekiel 36:33-35)

Imagine your waste places being rebuilt. Imagine the desolate non-productive aspects of your life now blooming and blossoming, like the Garden of Eden. Forgiveness means your iniquities will be remembered no more. This non-remembrance of our iniquities is repeated several times: *". . . their iniquities will I remember no more"* (Hebrews 8:12, 10:17; Revelation 18:5). It's time for another out loud, "Hallelujah!"

How wonderful, this forgiveness—and yet there is more!

**Iniquities Are Pardoned.**

Pardon is the cancellation of penalties and differs greatly from forgiveness. We get to forgive the trespasses of others, but we don't get to pardon them. They will still have to answer to God (and in some cases the laws of the land), even though we have forgiven them.

Pardon, the cancellation of penalties, can ONLY be granted by an official: one who has the power as executor of the laws. Since our iniquities are against God, it is only God who is legally qualified to issue a pardon. But this He does, praise The Lord! Notice from the Scripture cited above:

> *"I will cleanse them from all their **iniquity**,*
> *whereby they have sinned against me;*
> ***and I will pardon all their iniquities . . ."***

In the New Testament, this is referred to as the Doctrine of Remission. We know what happens when a disease is in remission: there is the disappearance or diminution of the signs and symptoms. In medical terms it can be partial or complete, temporary or permanent. Christ's blood is so vicariously effective that it provides for remission: *"For this is my blood of the new testament which is shed for the remission of sins"* (Matthew 26:28). Again the Scriptures say, *". . . without shedding of blood there is no remission"* (Hebrews 9:22).

Our Iniquities can be; 1) forgiven, 2) cleansed, and 3) pardoned. But these three are all contingent upon the fourth step, which is the condition for the first three.

**Iniquity Must Be Turned From**

The turning away from iniquity is one of the major reasons for the resurrection:

> *"Unto you first God,*
> *having **raised up his Son Jesus**,*
> *sent him to bless you,*
> ***in turning away every one of you from his iniquities.***"
> (Acts 3:26)

*". . . all this evil is come upon us:*
*yet made we not our prayer before the LORD our God,*
*that we might turn from our iniquities,*
*and understand thy truth."*
(Daniel 9:13)

Dearly Beloved, this is a most important part in your reading. With all that you have now learned about iniquity, are you ready and willing to turn, or be turned, from iniquity? You may be thinking that you don't have the power. If not, you will be given the power. That's why *"the turning"* is tied to the resurrection of our Lord. It means He is alive. He is here, and now with you, and He will empower you to turn. This is what He does best. But you must be willing. The contest of wills must end. Surrender. Surrender fully and absolutely. You can pray like Jeremiah who said, *"Turn thou me, and I shall be turned; for Thou art the Lord my God"* (Jeremiah 31:18).

# Chapter Twelve

## How To Terminate Present Iniquity

*"...mine iniquities*
*have taken hold upon me,*
*so that I am not able to look up;*
*they are more than the hairs of mine head:*
*therefore my heart faileth me.*

*Be pleased, O LORD,*
*to deliver me:*
*O LORD, make haste to help me."*
(Psalm 40:12-13)

We will not actually do anything without a sufficient and compelling motivation. This is especially true when the task at hand seems formidable. You have reviewed many truths in this book, and have hopefully come to the realization that iniquity has become an ingrained habit: a bondage with an all-encompassing grip on each of us. It's worse than being in prison. Instead of being behind the cold steel bars of a prison, it's like we carry these prison bars with us, everywhere we go. How shall we conquer? First we have to be adequately motivated. It's going to take more than positive thinking.

## How To Motivate Yourself

1. Review the benefits of conquering iniquity.
2. Review the temporal consequences of continuing in iniquity.
3. Review the eternal consequences of continuing in iniquity. Remember: *". . . depart from me . . . there shall be weeping and gnashing of teeth . . . and you yourselves thrust out . . ."* (Luke 13:27-28).
4. Realize how your iniquity affects God personally and directly.

## How Iniquity Affects God

Iniquity is God's number one enemy. It consists of our usurping God's rightful place in our lives. It makes us play god. It's what Satan did to become the enemy of God, and it got him eternally kicked out of heaven (see Luke 10:18). It was our iniquities that necessitated Jesus going to the cross. And it is the reason, while on the cross, Jesus felt the forsakenness of His Father: when our iniquities were being placed on Jesus, the Father turned His back. God stopped looking! Here's why:

> *"Thou art* of purer eyes than to behold evil,
> and canst not look on **iniquity**."
> (Habakkuk 1:13)

Iniquity separates us from God. *". . . your iniquities have separated between you and your God"* (Isaiah 59:2). I think it was A.W.Tozer who said we talk about God like we talk about jelly beans, with the same casualness. We think He is like us. When in fact, if we, like Isaiah in his iniquity-freeing moment, will see God properly, iniquity will be easy to break. Freedom begins when we see the vast distance between ourselves—the created—and The Creator. There is none like God!

> *"I saw also the Lord sitting upon a throne,*
> *high and lifted up, and his train filled the temple.*

*Above it stood the seraphims:*
*each one had six wings;*

*with twain he covered his face,*
*and with twain he covered his feet,*
*and with twain he did fly.*

*And one cried unto another, and said,*
*Holy, holy, holy, is the LORD of hosts:*
*the whole earth is full of his glory.*

*And the posts of the door moved*
*at the voice of him that cried,*
*and the house was filled with smoke.*

*Then said I, Woe is me! for I am undone;*
*because I am a man of unclean lips,*
*and I dwell in the midst of a people of unclean lips:*
*for mine eyes have seen the King, the LORD of hosts.*

*Then flew one of the seraphims unto me,*
*having a live coal in his hand,*
*which he had taken with the tongs from off the altar:*

*And he laid it upon my mouth, and said,*
*Lo, this hath touched thy lips;*
*and thine iniquity is taken away,*
*and thy sin purged."*
(Isaiah 6:1-7)

True worship is almost automatic. I speak not of the iniquitous worship of our day: the false fire, the offering up of what is designed to please ourselves and not God. Much contemporary worship is designed and calculated for human amusement and enjoyment, rather than for Divine acceptance. The fans, not the followers, arrive to enjoy the cheering, the camaraderie of the smoke and the dance, and the noise that resembles the "rock concert" Moses heard when coming down from the mountain of God. Joshua said, *"There is a noise of war in the camp."* On further inspection, Joshua clarified and said, it's *"... the noise of them that sing do I hear."* The tragic account of false worship continued: *"... as soon as he came nigh unto the camp, that he saw the calf, and the dancing: and Moses' anger waxed hot ..."* (Exodus 32:17-19).

Beloved, when we see the superiority and the holiness of the everlasting God, we will worship Him in spirit and in truth. While the world is filled with people being true to false gods, the church is filled with people being false to the true God. When we have to dress up worship to attract the fans, we are on the wrong track. *Ichabod*, which means the glory is departed (1 Samuel 4:21).

Worship is not for our benefit. In true worship, God is the audience. And we, the congregation, are to be the performers giving honor and glory and thanks to *"Him who sits on the throne."* Our praises are to be sung *"with understanding"* (Psalm 47:7). Both praise and worship are to be executed thoughtfully and intelligently, not intended to be tickling men's ears, but rather, adoring the Lord. It is to be didactic, instructive, and sensible; conveying the facts of God rather than our liking the sound of the music. The matter is more important than the music. In many a contemporary church service, the worship is designed to please ourselves, the pseudo-gods. And so we add the smoke and mirrors. *Ichabod*! All such self-pleasing in the name of "worship to God" is spurious, at best. God doesn't consider it worship at all.

But let's talk about you and me and holy motivation. The greatest righteous motivations you and I will ever have in this life will come from the realization that what we do affects God. We can grieve Him. Imagine that. Who could measure the depths of grief in the great heart of God, experienced because of us? Do we really know Him *"in the fellowship of His suffering?"* (Philippians 3:10).

Beloved, we can also bring pleasure to God. How I wish I could add ten extra pages to this book to write of this. You can bring happiness to God; so much so, that He will rejoice and sing about you!

*"The LORD thy God in the midst of thee is mighty;*
*he will save,*
*he will rejoice over thee with joy*
*he will rest in his love,*
*he will joy over thee with singing."*
(Zephaniah 3:17)

NOW we are motivated; motivated properly, purely, and righteously. We are motivated, because we can please God. And don't you think He's motivated to help you terminate iniquity? Now that we're motivated, what's next?

## Humble Yourself

Remember there are three fundamental dispositions. Each of us lives in one or the other.
1. Pride (thinking we are above others)
2. Humility (thinking we are equal with others)
3. Humiliation (thinking we are below others)

Pride, the inordinate and inflated sense of one's own status, drives most of us. Pride is the consequential attitude or disposition of iniquity. It is a core issue. In the historical account of Sodom and Gomorrah, we see the direct association between iniquity and pride: *"Behold, this was the iniquity of thy sister Sodom, pride . . ."* (Ezekiel 16:49). Pride has compelling powers. It also has consequences. Here is a list of some of the consequences of pride.

1. Pride enslaves to wrong behavioral patterns and attitudes: *"Pride compasseth them about as a chain"* (Psalm 73:6).

2. Pride causes verbal abuse: *"In the mouth of the foolish is a rod of pride: but the lips of the wise shall preserve them"* (Proverbs 14:3).

   *"For the sin of their mouth and the words of their lips let them even be taken in their pride: and for cursing and lying which they speak"* (Psalm 59:12).

3. Pride causes contention with others: *"Only by pride cometh contention: but with the well advised is wisdom"* (Proverbs 13:10).

4. Pride causes shame and a lack of wisdom: *"When pride cometh, then cometh shame: but with the lowly is wisdom"* (Proverbs 11:2).

5. Pride precedes failure: *"Pride goeth before destruction, and an haughty spirit before a fall"* (Proverbs 16:18).

6. Pride is repulsive to others: *"A man's pride shall bring him low: but honour shall uphold the humble in spirit"* (Proverbs 29:23).

7. Pride causes lying and misrepresentation: "... *he is* very proud: *even* of his haughtiness, and his pride, and his wrath: *but* his lies *shall* not *be* so" (Isaiah 16:6).

8. Pride causes self-deception: *"The pride of thine heart hath deceived thee... Though thou exalt thyself as the eagle, and though thou set thy nest among the stars, thence will I bring thee down, saith the Lord"* (Obadiah 1:3-4).

   *"For if a man think himself to be something, when he is nothing, he deceiveth himself"* (Galatians 6:3).

9. Pride causes self-destructive behaviors: *"Woe to the crown of pride, to the drunkards of Ephraim, whose glorious beauty is a fading flower . . ."* (Isaiah 28:1).

10. Pride causes severe self-exaltation: *"We have heard the pride of Moab, (he is exceeding proud) his loftiness, and his arrogancy, and his pride, and the haughtiness of his heart"* (Jeremiah 48:29).

11. Pride destroys family members: *"The Lord will destroy the house of the proud"* (Proverbs 15:25).

12. Pride causes the abandonment of facts: *"Most men will proclaim every one his own goodness: but a faithful man who can find?"* (Proverbs 20:6).

13. Pride prevents seeking after God: *"The wicked, through the pride of his countenance, will not seek after God: God is not in all his thoughts"* (Psalm 10:4).

14. Pride crowds out all thoughts about God: *"The wicked, through the pride of his countenance, will not seek after God: God is not in all his thoughts"* (Psalm 10:4).

15. Pride is not to be trusted: *"Blessed is that man that maketh the LORD his trust, and respecteth not the proud, nor such as turn aside to lies"* (Psalm 40:4).

16. Pride causes the rejection of God's commandments: *"Thou hast rebuked the proud that are cursed, which do err from thy commandments"* (Psalm 119:21).

17. Pride causes vengeance: *"Proud and haughty scorner is his name, who dealeth in proud wrath"* (Proverbs 21:24).

18. Pride creates distance from God: *"Though the LORD be high, yet hath he respect unto the lowly: but the proud he knoweth afar off"* (Psalm 138:6).

19. Pride is an adequate cause for God's hatred: *"Every one that is proud in heart is an abomination to the LORD: though hand join in hand, he shall not be unpunished"* (Proverbs 16:5).

20. Pride causes trouble-making: *"He that is of a proud heart stirreth up strife . . ."* (Proverbs 28:25).

21. Pride creates a false sense of success: *"And now we call the proud happy . . ."* (Malachi 3:15).

22. Pride creates delusions of grandeur: *". . . he hath scattered the proud in the imagination of their hearts"* (Luke 1:51).

23. Pride creates pseudo-intellectualism: *"He is proud, knowing nothing, but doting about questions and strifes of words, whereof cometh envy, strife, railings, evil surmisings, Perverse disputings of men of corrupt minds, and destitute of the truth, supposing that gain is godliness: from such withdraw thyself"* (1 Timothy 6:4-5).

24. Pride prevents the fear of God: *"The fear of the Lord is to hate evil: pride, and arrogancy, and the evil way, and the froward mouth"* (Proverbs 8:13).

25. Pride causes Divine resistance: *"God resisteth the proud, and giveth grace to the humble"* (1 Peter 5:5).

This list should help us see clearly that pride, the attitude of iniquity, is wicked, repulsive, and disgusting. The question for each of us now becomes what to do about this innate condition. Here is the Biblical answer:

*"Humble yourselves in the sight of the Lord,*
*And He shall lift you up."*
*(James 4:10)*

*"Humble yourselves therefore*
*under the mighty hand of God,*
*That He may exalt you in due time:*

*Casting all your care upon Him;*
*For He careth for you."*
(1 Peter 5:6-7)

### How To Humble Ourselves

We must first be utterly persuaded that humility, and not pride, is the worthy pursuit. And that humility does *not* mean humiliation.

Secondly, we must realize that we are personally responsible for this achievement. Let us humble ourselves, so that neither God nor others will have to. It is our task.

Thirdly, we must have the end in view; and it is quite delightful. God will lift us up to what we should be. He will exalt us at the right time. Then we will be secure. We will not have to get to the proper station in life through manipulation, politics, self-promotion, or artificial means:

> *". . . be clothed with humility:*
> *for God resisteth the proud,*
> *and giveth grace to the humble."*
> (1 Peter 5:5)

God will now give grace. When God places us, we will not be vulnerable to the attacks of others:

> *"Promotion cometh neither from the east, nor the west,*
> *nor from the south. But God is the judge:*
>
> *He putteth one down, and setteth up another."*
> (Psalm 75:6-7)

Fourthly, when we humble ourselves we get to *"cast all our care upon Him"* (1 Peter 5:7). What is that worth? Notice in the Scripture above, that when we humble ourselves under the hand of God, that He assumes responsibility for our well-being. This is strongly indicated by the phrase, *"For He careth for you."*

Fifthly, there are a number of Biblically authorized activities which can help us humble ourselves. They may seem mechanical, but believe me, they have many spiritual dynamics embedded in them. Here are ten of them:

1) Confess your faults to caring others, and ask them to pray for you: *"Confess your faults one to another, and pray for one another, that ye may be healed"* (James 5:16).

2) Stay submitted to the proper authorities. Pride forces us to think we are the final authority.

3) Ask for forgiveness. Go to those you have wronged (no letters or phone calls), work out the wording in advance, and ask for forgiveness. This is not an apology. It should go something like this: "I was so wrong when I (said or did thus and so) and I know I don't deserve forgiveness, but would you be willing to forgive me?"

4) Make restitution. We can make our wrongs *right*; but we can never make right all the consequences of our wrongs. Nevertheless, if I stole a car yesterday and I repent today, what should I do? Answer: take the car back. What if I stole the car seven years ago? What if it wasn't a car but a piece of cheap jewelry? The Scriptures say, *"He that covereth his sins shall not prosper: but whoso confesseth and forsaketh them shall have mercy"* (Proverbs 28:13). When Zacchaeus told the Lord that he would restore four times as much to those he had taken from by false accusation, the Lord said, *"This day is salvation come to this house"* (Luke 19:8-9). Restitution is the proof of repentance.

5) Return good for evil. Pride wants us to give evil for evil and perhaps good for good. But we don't respond according to an exalted ego anymore (see Matthew 5:44-45).

6) Welcome criticism, even if it comes from hypocrites or from people whose intentions may be evil. *"Bless them which persecute you: bless and curse not"* (Romans 12:14). Remarkably, Jesus told us to listen to hypocrites and to obey them. He told us not to follow their example, however: *"All therefore whatsoever they bid you observe, that observe and do; but do not ye after their works for they say and do not"* (Matthew 23:3). (When my wife read this part of the manuscript she hand wrote in, "Be sure to tell them to welcome criticisms from their wife as well." There I did it. . . sort of.)

7) Kneel before the Lord. Kneeling is a body position that shows reverence, submission, and obeisance. It is a bowing down, a prostration before the Lord. The word *proskynein,* occurs fifty-nine times in the New Testament. Liturgical churches carry on the tradition. *"Let us kneel before the Lord, Our Maker..."* (Psalm 95:6). Let our knees bow before the One whose name is above all names.

8) Give credit to others. Give honor to whom it is due.

9) Express gratefulness, making known to God and others the many ways they have benefited our lives.

10) Give sacrificially as an expression of gratefulness to God for all the benefits He has given to you.

## Obey Every Instruction of the Lord

The passage regarding the transmission of iniquities from fathers to children provides a dynamic insight to iniquity, termination, and prevention. That Scripture speaks of *"... visiting the iniquity of the fathers upon the children unto the third and fourth generation of them that hate me. And showing mercy unto thousands of them that love me and keep my commandments"* (Deuteronomy 5:9-10).

Notice that the antidote, the counteracting measures against the passed-on effects of iniquity, are two-fold: love for God and the keeping of His commandments.

I recall the nightmarish war, the combat I had in struggling to deal with my iniquity. I had great consternation over the potential effects of my iniquity on our two daughters. I needed to deal with iniquity, not just for my soul's sake, but for their sakes. I needed to be loving God and keeping His commandments.

I am pleased to report to you that our two daughters have become awesome before the Lord. I claim no credit. Each of them has been a seeker of the Lord and His ways. They married men of the same stripe. Over several decades now they have disciplined themselves and proven true to the Lord and His Word. I'm also sure that they benefited from the virtues of their mother. They are spectacular; they are heroes of mine. And I see their children being raised in an iniquity-free environment.

Commands are simply instructions. They are, however, instructions that are so important they have benefits and consequences attached to them: benefits if we follow them and consequences if we don't. They are designed, and have forged into them, the dynamics of success.

# Chapter Thirteen

# How To Prevent
# Future Iniquity

*"Let every one
that nameth the name of Christ
depart from iniquity. "*
(2 Timothy 2:19)

## 1. Get back what iniquity has taken: *"First Love"*

Iniquity is the enemy of love. The opposite of love is not hate. For example, true love requires hatred: hatred of evil. Love is giving to God and others without personal profit as a motive. Iniquity is taking from God and others, regardless of the expense to them. Love is giving; iniquity and selfishness are about taking.

The greatest of commandments is to *"Love the Lord, Thy God with all thine heart, and with all thy soul, and with all thy might"* (Deuteronomy 6:5). The created greatly adoring the Creator, is quite normal. But we, all of us, have gone our own ways, ignored Him, forsaken Him, deserted Him, and have settled for playing God ourselves. That never works out. Some of us have returned to the Lord, and He has graciously pardoned us. We returned by following the instructions in Isaiah fifty-five:

*"Seek ye the LORD while he may be found,*
*call ye upon him while he is near:*

*Let the wicked forsake his way,*
*and the unrighteous man his thoughts:*
*and let him return unto the LORD,*
*and he will have mercy upon him;*
*and to our God, for he will abundantly pardon."*
(Isaiah 55:6-7)

1. We sought Him while He could be found.
2. We called upon Him while He was near.
3. We forsook our wicked ways.
4. We left off our unrighteous way of thinking.
5. We returned to the Lord.
6. He had mercy on us.
7. He abundantly pardoned us.

Thus began the greatest romance of a lifetime (yea, an eternity), a love relationship with God. It was intense. It was passionate. It was as if the fires of love burned within us. Passion for Him was normal. We sought Him. He responded. We cried. He dried our tears. Our sorrows were turned into laughter. We walked with Him. Consulted the great, *I Am*. Enthusiasm abounded. Doing right became our ultimate intention. We lived to please Him. His smile inspired us. His voice was sweet. We met Him in secret places. Our fellowship with Him was unbroken. Beloved Reader, I hope you experienced this *"first love"* with Him. More importantly, I hope you are still in love with Him now. If not, iniquity has taken away that zeal, that passion, that first love:

*"And because **iniquity** shall abound,*
*the love of many shall wax cold."*
(Matthew 24:12)

No one can go two different directions at the same time. Jesus gave us an example when He said, *"No man can serve two masters: for either he will hate the one, and love the other; or else he will hold to the one, and despise the other. . ."* (Matthew 6:24). You may not hate God, but notice the *or else* condition: *"he will hold to the one and despise the other."* We get complacent. His instructions become interfering. God's commands always interfere with selfishness and iniquity. The danger is that we *"wax cold."*

Don't get me wrong. We still hate evil, speak out against hypocrisy, do good works (even with zeal), and attend the meetings. We keep going forward, it seems. But! But! But we have lost our *"first love."* This was the exact description of the Church in Ephesus in Revelation Chapter Two:

> *"I know thy works, and thy labour, and thy patience,*
> *and how thou canst not bear them which are evil:*
> *and thou hast tried them which say they are apostles,*
> *and are not, and hast found them liars:*
>
> *And hast borne, and hast patience,*
> *and for my name's sake hast laboured,*
> *and hast not fainted.*
>
> *Nevertheless I have somewhat against thee,*
> *because thou hast **left thy first love.** "*
> (Revelations 2:2-4)

**How To Test For *"First Love"***

1. I have more delight in the Lord than in anyone else: *"Love the Lord with all your **heart** . . ."* (See Deuteronomy 6:5, quoted above, for points 1-4).

2. I long for time with Him in prayer and in His Word: *"Love the Lord with all your **soul** . . ."* (I recently read this: "Complaining about the silence of God with your Bible closed is like complaining about not getting texts when your phone is turned off").

3. During leisure moments I reflect on the Lord: *"Love the Lord with all your **mind** ..."*

4. I do not do the things that displease the Lord: *"Love the Lord with all your **strength** ..."*

5. I keep all His commandments: *"If ye **keep** my commandments, ye shall abide in my love"* (John 15:10).

6. I treat Christian brothers and sisters as I do the Lord: *"By this shall all men know you are my disciples, if you have **love** one to another"* (John 13:35).

7. I view His commandments as His loving instructions, not as restrictions to my happiness: *"For this is the love of God, that we keep His commandments: and His commandments are not grievous"* (1 John 5:3).

8. I care about the approval of God rather that the opinions of any others: *"How can ye believe, which receive honour one of another, and seek not the honour that cometh from God only?"* (John 5:44).

9. I am careful not to do any activity that offends or weakens a fellow Christian; such would be a sin against Christ Himself: *"But take heed lest by any means this liberty of yours become a stumblingblock to them that are weak... But when ye sin so against the brethren, and wound their weak conscience, ye sin against Christ"* (1 Corinthians 8:9, 12).

10. I weep over the sinful condition of mankind. Aching with disappointment, Jesus says, *"... ye will not come to me, that ye might have life"* (John 5:40). To me, this is one of the saddest verses in the Bible.

11. I feel the feelings of God. Love causes our feelings to be synced with God's. Whatever is on God's heart will be on our hearts also, if indeed we love Him. For example, because of His love, this is how God feels toward us. He is, *"touched with the feeling of our*

*infirmities . . . "* (Hebrews 4:15). On the other hand, there are those, *"who being past feeling have given themselves over . . . "* to other pursuits (Ephesians 4:19).

12. I enter into both His power and His sufferings. Genuine love suffers, and according to the famous love chapter of the Bible, it suffers long: *"That I might know Him, and the power of His resurrection, and the fellowship of His sufferings . . . "* (Philippians 3:10).

**How To Get Back Your "First Love"**

Following the Revelation chapter two passage above, where the Lord awakens us to our loss of *"first love,"* He gives us three steps in the next verse—verse five— to change the loss and enable us to recover our *"first love:"*

1. *"**Remember** therefore from whence thou art fallen:"* We must realize that it was we who moved, we who changed the relationship, we who lost. So we need to remember how it was and how it still should be. We make the *"first love"* condition the utmost pursuit of our lives.

2. *"And **repent:**"* We must repent of the iniquity of allowing whoever or whatever to capture our affections away from Him.

3. *" . . . And **do the first works**"*: Spend time with Him. Delight yourself in Him. Refuse distractions. Watch out for amusements which cause the meaningless passage of time. Make Him your *"first love."*

**2. Develop Genuine, Joyful Self-Acceptance**

Genuine self-acceptance keeps us right where we should be: living in humility, with no self-exaltation necessary or even desirable, and certainly no humiliation or self-rejection. How do we arrive at genuine and joyful self-acceptance?

1. Realize that God, the Creator, made you! Did you get that? Think about it for a moment. This wonderful being of God created elephants

that stand on their feet for forty years, eat 200-400 pounds of vege-
tation a day, have molars that are twelve inches long and four inches
wide, have hearts that weigh forty-five pounds, and communicate at
frequencies below what the human ear can hear. God also created
termites that live up to thirty years (but hopefully not in your house);
woodpeckers that peck twenty times per second without knocking
their brains out; bees that flap their wings 300 times a second, which
is faster the an airplane propeller turns; flamingos that can only eat
when their heads are upside down; frogs that have to close their eyes
to swallow; rabbits which talk to each other by thumping their feet;
earthworms that have neither eyes nor ears; ants that never sleep and
have five noses; ducks that frequently swim while sleeping; polar
bears that are all lefties; hummingbirds that weigh less than a penny
and can fly backwards or hover; pigeons whose feathers weigh more
than their bones; cows that chew eighteen hours per day; horses that
can look forward with one eye and backwards with their other eye
at the same time; adult moths that never eat; owls that can't move
their eyes; insects whose blood is yellow; lions whose roar can be
heard as far as five miles away; whales and dolphins that fall only
half asleep, because the two hemispheres of their brains take turns
sleeping, so that the half of their brain that is awake can make sure
they continue going to the surface to breathe.

2. God created you as well, and He is a marvelous Creator with
diversity that is infinite: there are no two snowflakes alike, no two
finger prints alike, and no two people alike. He made you absolutely
unique, not a clone, not a copy but an original, a first edition. Here's
the proof: *"Know ye that the Lord He is God: it is He that hath made
us and not we ourselves; we are His people . . ."* (Psalm 100:3).

A man and a woman got together, your father and your mother, and
in keeping with the laws that God designed, there was going to be
a baby coming: *you.* But who put the *you* inside that baby's body?
The answer is God. People can make babies, but they cannot make
people. You are a spirit. That's why you have two fathers: a father
after the flesh and The Father who made you, the spirit. So Jesus

taught us to pray, *"Our Father which art in heaven"* (Matthew 6:9). The father of the real you is God: *". . . we have had fathers of our flesh which corrected us, and we gave them reverence: shall we not much rather be in subjection unto the **Father of spirits** . . .?"* (Hebrews 12:9).

3. He made the real you, specifically, and He doesn't make mistakes. You are His workmanship. Iniquity causes us to try to be someone or something else. You will be in deep trouble if you don't accept yourself. This trouble will last the rest of your life and keep you perpetually on the wrong track: *"Woe unto him that striveth with his Maker! Shall the clay say to him that fashioneth it, What makest Thou?"* (Isaiah 45:9). Give yourself a treat, and read, ponder, and meditate on the first eighteen verses of Psalm 139. This is the story of the real you. Stop trying to be anyone or anything else.

4. Stop comparing yourself with others. I know. I know. The culture has already promoted this from grade school to college, from advertising to beauty competitions. But it is devastating in its consequences. *"We dare not . . ."* Did you get that? *"We dare not make ourselves of the number or compare ourselves with some that commend themselves: but they measuring themselves by themselves, and comparing themselves among themselves are not wise"* (2 Corinthians 10:12). I know that's a mouthful. But break it down: A) Don't be a part of the group that compares themselves. Watch out. It's the talk of the locker room and the talk shows; it's everywhere. B) They commend themselves; they praise themselves. They are their own Public Relations firm. C) This is not a wise enterprise. It comes down to everyone flaunting their iniquity. Don't join in the competition. It's not smart.

5. Celebrate, but don't boast about the real you. Iniquity causes boasting: *"How long shall they utter and speak hard things? And all the workers of iniquity boast themselves"* (Psalm 94:4). The very next verse explains the consequences: *"They break in pieces thy people. . ."* If you want to boast, boast about God (Psalm 44:8). Be sure to celebrate you. You really are a somebody!

6. Avoid competition. Competition pits you against others and others against you. Competition is a contest. The obsession with sports today needs to be questioned. When two fighters enter the ring, there is going to be a winner and a loser. What is happening in the audience or to the viewers? Don't they end up rejoicing in iniquity? We get excited about one punching out the lights of the other. This same condition of strife carries over in most walks of life. Businesses compete. Schools compete. Churches compete. Nations compete. Why are we always trying to outdo one another? What can end the strife? Can't we help one another? Perhaps we are marching to the wrong beat.

### 3. Return To Submission To Your Rightful Authorities

Remember that Iniquity manifests itself in the following ways:
Exaltation of self (Intoxication)
Exaltation of self above or equal to God
Exaltation of self above or equal to authorities
Exaltation of self above others
Refusal to accept one's value or station in life
Refusal to be what God says one should be
Refusal to do what God says one should do

Iniquity often manifests itself in stirring up rebellion against authorities. The Biblical term is insurrection.

*"Hide me from the secret counsel of the wicked;*
*from **the insurrection of the workers of iniquity:"***
(Psalm 64:2)

In order to return to the proper relationship to your authorities, you should consider the following:

1. Determine who your rightful authorities are.

2. Remember that each rightful authority has a specified jurisdiction, a defined scope, and measured parameters; and must operate within the specified dimensions.

3. Go to each of your authorities and ask forgiveness for not having honored their God-assigned leadership in your life, and pledge to respond properly, going forward.

4. Consider the authority roles of parents, employers, civil authorities, church elders, and tutors.

## 4. Develop a Servant Spirit

I told you earlier that there are a thousand things I love about God. I've never counted them or even listed them (yet). Some of them are so profound; staggeringly so. Certainly you've read a few of them within these pages. However, consider this: God, in a very large measure, is a servant God, a servant Father, a servant King. He cares about His subjects. We know what God is like, through Jesus. Jesus is the visible image of the invisible God. Whatever Jesus is like, God the Father is like; whatever Jesus is like, the Holy Spirit is like. Jesus has a servant-spirit. He Himself said, *". . . the son of man came not to be ministered unto, but to minister . . ."* (Matthew 20:28). He came not to be served, but to serve. Further, Jesus taught that a servant-spirit was the essence of greatness:

> *"But he that is greatest among you shall be your servant.*
>
> *And whosoever shall exalt himself shall be abased;*
> *and he that shall humble himself shall be exalted."*
> (Matthew 23:11-12)

This is stunning: Jesus, a servant. If I were God coming to earth, I think I'd have hired a PR firm to spread the word ahead of time. I would have at least had celestial loud speakers, a back-up band, a parade, a white horse, and ten thousand-plus attendees. I'd have tried to make a big splash with colored brochures and massive banners, and made sure to have crack reporters and Fox news on hand.

But not Jesus. Some angels did show up, but there were no crowds for them. There were just a few smelly shepherds and some sheep in an out-of-the-way, remote location. And to show up as a babe?

I guess when you are God, you can do such things. No need to impress anyone when you're God Almighty.

He wasn't just a king. He was a Servant King. Imagine! He washed the feet of His disciples. And He was always helping someone, always doing good deeds, always healing, always blessing children, always caring, always going out of His way—for others.

Then it came to dying, not for Himself, but for others! And who were the others? You'd think they'd be the nice people, the important people, the nobility, or at least those who were friendly toward Him. But no. Not Jesus. Not God. He died for His enemies: *"For while we were yet sinners, Christ died for us"* (Romans 5:8). Do you know what that means? If you were at war, in a foxhole shooting across a field at the enemy, and a grenade landed in the foxhole, a fellow soldier might jump on it, dying to save a comrade. But Jesus died for those on the other side of the field shooting at Him. Yes, He died for His enemies.

**How to develop a servant spirit**

1. Let the Lord Jesus Christ be your model and example.

a. Become others-conscious: *"Look not every man on his own things, but every man also on the things of others"* (Philippians 2:4).

b. Learn to think as He thinks: *"Let this mind be in you, which was also in Christ Jesus . . ."* (Philippians 2:5).

c. Don't concern yourself with your reputation: *"But made Himself of no reputation . . ."* (Philippians 2:7).

d. Look and act like a servant, instead of a boss: *". . . and took upon Himself the form of a servant . . ."* (Philippians 2:7).

e. Keep humble. You serve from beneath, not from above: *"And being found in fashion as a man, He humbled Himself . . ."* (Philippians 2:8).

f. Learn to obey the instructions of those you are serving: *". . . and became obedient unto death, even the death of the cross"* (Philippians 2:8).

2. Recognize that greatness is based on how many and how well you serve others, not on how many serve you: *"And whosoever of you will be the chiefest, shall be servant of all"* (Mark 10:44).

3. Don't get in the lordship position. The Gentiles wanted to rule and be bosses over the people. They thought greatness was based on how many you could dominate or rule over. But watch Jesus's instructions:

*"But Jesus called them to him, and saith unto them,*
*Ye know that they which are accounted to rule over the Gentiles*
*exercise lordship over them;*
*and their great ones exercise authority upon them.*

*But **so shall it not be among you**:*
*but whosoever will be great among you,*
*shall be your minister:*

*And whosoever of you will be the chiefest,*
*shall be servant of all.*

*For even the Son of man came not to be ministered unto,*
*but to minister, and to give his life a ransom for many."*
(Mark 10:42-45)

Jesus made it plain: "Don't be bossy. Don't try to be lord over others. Instead seek to serve.

4. Realize that the way to serve Christ is to serve others; but it is Christ we serve, not men:

*"Ye are bought with a price;*
*be not ye the servants of men."*
(1 Corinthians 7:23)

Here is a great parable that Jesus used to demonstrate that serving others can be serving Him.

> *"Then shall the King say unto them on his right hand,*
> *Come, ye blessed of my Father, inherit the kingdom*
> *prepared for you from the foundation of the world:*
>
> *For I was an hungred, and ye gave me meat:*
> *was thirsty, and ye gave me drink:*
> *I was a stranger, and ye took me in:*
>
> *Naked, and ye clothed me:*
> *I was sick, and ye visited me:*
> *I was in prison, and ye came unto me.*
>
> *Then shall the righteous answer him, saying,*
> *Lord, when saw we thee an hungred, and fed thee?*
> *or thirsty, and gave thee drink?*
>
> *When saw we thee a stranger, and took thee in?*
> *or naked, and clothed thee?*
>
> *Or when saw we thee sick,*
> *or in prison, and came unto thee?*
>
> *And the King shall answer and say unto them,*
> *Verily I say unto you,*
> *Inasmuch as ye have done it unto one of the least*
> *of these my brethren, ye have done it unto me."*
> (Matthew 25:34-40)

5. Do not look for honor from men:

> *"How can ye believe,*
> *which receive honour one from another;*
> *and seek not the honour that cometh from God only?"*
> (John 5:44)

Seek only to please the Lord. To your own Master only, do you rise or fall. God's approbation is all you need: *"Who art thou that judgest another man's servant? To his own master he standeth or falleth. Yea, he shall be holden up: for God is able to make him stand"* (Romans 14:4).

6. Learn to esteem others.

*"Let nothing be done through strife or vainglory;*
*but in lowliness of mind let each esteem other better than themselves.*

*Look not every man on his own things,*
*but every man also on the things of others."*
(Phillippians 2:3-4)

## 5. Live Love

Love is the antithesis of iniquity. In the famous love chapter of the Bible, love stands out in bold contrast to iniquity:

*"(Love) rejoiceth not in inquity . . ."*
(1 Corinthians 13:6)

We know that *"God is love"* (1 John 4:8). If love and iniquity are incompatible, then we know that God, since He IS love, does not have any iniquity. But let's be sure, according to the Scriptures:

*"Wherefore now let the fear of the LORD be upon you;*
*take heed and do it:*
*for there is no iniquity with the LORD our God,*
*nor respect of persons, nor taking of gifts."*
(2 Chronicles 19:7)

God loves you. The very best theology that has ever been presented was in the little Sunday School chorus, "Jesus loves me, this I know, for the Bible tells me so." God loves, and God is loving. His goal is to make us into ladies and gentlemen who love. In fact, it's the proof of being a genuine Christian. *"By this shall all men know that ye are my disciples, if ye have love one to another"* (John 13:35).

Living love is the ultimate lifestyle of God. It's what He's looking for in His children. It is the main character quality produced in us by His grace. It's a quality that He intends to eternalize, that is, to give eternal life to, so that heaven stays heaven. Iniquity was kicked out of heaven. Iniquity must be confined and restricted. Otherwise, it would contaminate the whole universe. So there really is a hell, a place of confinement, the Alcatraz of Eternity. It is like an insane asylum with rubber walls, where selfishness cannot damage others or the rest of God's universe; where the fires of unfulfillment burn on forever, because selfishness and iniquity are unsustainable and insatiable. It reaches out to grab, clutch, and grasp but comes up empty. But you and I, Beloved, are destined to live love, the opposite of selfishness and iniquity. Here's how.

**What it means to "live love"** (1 Corinthians 13:4-8):

1. Be willing to suffer: *"Charity suffereth long . . ."*

2. Be kind to those who cause your suffering: *"Charity suffereth long, and is kind . . ."*

3. Refuse to be envious: *"Charity envieth not . . ."*

4. Refuse to compare or compete with others: *"Charity vaunteth not itself . . ."*

5. Refuse to exalt yourself: *"(Charity) is not puffed up . . ."*

6. Insist on reverencing others, refusing to display bad manners: *"Doth not behave itself unseemly . . ."*

7. Insist on choosing what is best for others, without regard for personal benefit: *"Seeketh not her own . . ."*

8. Refuse to be irritated in your agenda: *"Is not easily provoked . . ."*

9. Be careful to maintain loving mental attitudes: *"Thinketh no evil . . ."*

10. Mourn over inequalities: *"Rejoiceth not in iniquity . . ."*

11. Insist on honesty, authenticity, transparency, openness, and spontaneity: *"But rejoiceth in the truth . . ."*

12. Be willing to assume responsibilities: *"Beareth all things . . ."*

13. Keep full trust in others until it is no longer factually possible to do so: *"Believeth all things . . ."*

14. Maintain optimism, because you understand the superiority of love over iniquity: *"Hopeth all things . . ."*

15. Stay fortified to the point of being undaunted: *"Endureth all things"*

The qualities of love will always defeat iniquity, because *"Love never faileth."*

## 6. Develop a merciful disposition

Iniquity is so set on it's own self interest that showing mercy to others doesn't occur in it's thinking. Iniquity is not soft or gentle, compassionate or caring towards others.

Clearly the Scriptures explain that developing the character quality of mercy helps to rid us of iniquity.

> *"By mercy and truth **iniquity** is purged:*
> *and by the fear of the LORD men depart from evil."*
> (Proverbs 16:6)

Had Nebuchadnezzar heeded the wise counsel of Daniel, he would not have gone crazy, ending up eating grass like a beast in the field. He slept in the damp and the dew of each night. His hair was tattered and mangled grown to the length of eagle's feathers and his fingernails were like bird's claws. Deranged and out of his mind simply because he harkened not to this instruction. He chose sin and iniquity over tranquillity.

*"...O king, let my counsel be acceptable unto thee,*
*and break off thy sins by righteousness,*
*and thine **iniquities** by shewing mercy to the poor;*
*if it may be a lengthening of thy tranquillity."*
(Daniel 4:27)

# CHAPTER FOURTEEN

## How We Overcome
## The Iniquities
## Of Our Fathers

*"Our fathers have sinned,*
*and are not;*
*and we have borne their iniquities."*
(Lamentations 5:7)

**Iniquities are passed to us from our fathers.**

The Scriptures are very clear that we must deal with not only our own iniquities, but those passed to us by our fathers. At least four passages assert the fact that iniquities can be passed on and affect children three to four generations later. These passages are oft misquoted as "the sins of the fathers are passed on." Let's look carefully at these passages.

> *". . . for I the LORD thy God am a jealous God,*
> *visiting the **iniquity of the fathers***
> *upon the children unto the third and fourth*
> *generation of them that hate me;*

*And shewing mercy unto thousands*
*of them that love me,*
*and keep my commandments."*
(Exodus 20:5-6 and Deuteronomy 5:9-10)

**Iniquities are passed on to those who hate God, not to those who love Him and keep his commandments.**

Iniquities of fathers are passed on to *"them that hate me."* But mercy is shown unto *"them that love me, and keep my commandments."* Love for God has many benefits, as does the keeping of His commandments. One of the benefits, according to the above text, appears to be the nullifying of the effects of our father's iniquities. Love for God is always demonstrated in keeping His commandments and doing so joyfully:

*"For this is the love of God,*
*that we keep his commandments:*
*and his commandments are not grievous."*
(1 John 5:3)

Keeping the Lord's commandments is proof that we really love Him. In fact, if a person does not keep His commandments, he evidences that he does not love God and that he is lying if he says he does:

*"And hereby we do know that we know him,*
*if we keep his commandments.*

*He that saith, I know him,*
*and keepeth not his commandments,*
*is a liar, and the truth is not in him.*

*But whoso keepeth his word,*
*in him verily is the love of God perfected:*
*hereby know we that we are in him."*
(1 John 2:3-5)

**God is intent on forgiving iniquity when He can wisely do so.**

The predisposition of the Lord is to be merciful, gracious, longsuffering, and full of goodness and truth; and as you will see in the following text, these qualities lead to forgiving iniquity. However, He will not clear the guilty, visiting the iniquity of their fathers upon them. This is a reinforcement of the previous text. Who are the non-guilty? Those who love Him and keep His commandments. Let's allow the Scriptures to speak for themselves:

> *"And the LORD passed by before him,*
> *and proclaimed, The LORD, The LORD God,*
> *merciful and gracious, longsuffering*
> *and abundant in goodness and truth,*
>
> *Keeping mercy for thousands,*
> ***forgiving iniquity*** *and transgression and sin,*
> *and that will by no means clear the guilty;*
> *visiting the **iniquity of the fathers upon the children**,*
> *and upon the children's children,*
> *unto the third and to the fourth generation."*
> (Exodus 34:6-7)

Again in the following passage we have the same principles reiterated. I hope you are not disappointed in the frequent, if not constant, quoting and inclusion of full passages of Scripture in this book. The truth is that the Scriptures are the most important part of the book.

> *"The LORD is longsuffering, and of great mercy,*
> *forgiving iniquity and transgression,*
> *and by no means clearing the guilty,*
> *visiting **the iniquity of the fathers upon the children***
> ***unto the third and fourth generation.***

*Pardon, I beseech thee,*
*the **iniquity** of this people*
*according unto the greatness of thy mercy*
*and as thou hast forgiven this people,*
*from Egypt even until now."*
(Numbers 14:18-19)

## Iniquities are passed to us by our fathers, not our mothers.

It should be noted that nowhere do we find that the iniquities of our mothers are passed on to us. What could be the reason? Perhaps it is because the father is the legal (God-ordained) authority in the home. He is the leader. And as the leader goes, so go the followers.

The Scriptures give no indication that the method of transmitting the iniquities of the fathers to their children is through the blood. In fact, quite the contrary. Every passage indicates that the iniquities are *"visited upon."* They come from His leadership and example and from his motivations and patterns of behavior.

## What about the sins of our fathers?

The responsibility for our sin is our own. This text is clear that each of us shall die for our own sins and not for those of another. Further, the text says that the children shall not pay the price for their fathers' sins. You do not have to deal with your father's sins, only his iniquities:

*"But he slew not their children,*
*but did as it is written in the law in the book of Moses,*
*where the LORD commanded, saying,*
*The fathers shall not die for the children,*
*neither shall the children die for the fathers,*
*but every man shall die for his own sin."*
(2 Chronicles 25:4)

*"The fathers shall not be put to death for the children,*
*neither shall the children be put to death for the fathers:*
*every man shall be put to death for his own sin."*
(Deuteronomy 24:16)

**Iniquity in the heart produces iniquities in behavior.**

Iniquity is a heart condition, as we shall see more clearly in the next chapter. This condition of the heart produces both sins and iniquities. It is the heart that must be dealt with in order to effect a lasting termination of this iniquitous condition:

*"For out of the heart proceed evil thoughts,*
*murders, adulteries, fornications,*
*thefts, false witness, blasphemies:*

*These are the things which defile a man . . ."*
(Matthew 15:19-20)

**The following is a list of the possible iniquities, passed on from your father, which you may have to deal with:**

**1. How your father treated his wife**

If your father treated his wife, your mother, in any manner which was unequal to the love and dignity to which she should have been treated (as defined by the Scriptures), you will be visited with this same iniquity. You will have the tendency to treat your wife iniquitously, which is unequal to how she should be treated. You must now deal with this iniquity visited upon you from your father. How can you tell if you or your father are not treating your wives properly? Knowing the *Seven Instructions For Husbands* (see Appendix Four) will answer that question. If you are a daughter, the iniquity visited upon you will be to accept unloving, undignified treatment, which leads to the acceptance of abuse to one degree or another.

## 2. How your father treated you

If your father treated you in a manner unequal to how a father should treat his children (as defined by the Scriptures), you will be visited with this same iniquity. You will have the tendency to treat your children iniquitously, which is unequal to how they should be treated, and you must now deal with this iniquity visited upon you from your father. If he provoked you, you will probably provoke your children. If he dealt with you angrily or harshly, you will naturally do the same. Now you will need to learn the Biblical principles of parenting and implement them in order to overcome this iniquity that came from your father. And you will need to develop disciplines to counteract the tendency towards such in-equities.

Can you see from the above two illustrations how loving God and keeping his commandments prevents the iniquity of your father from coming upon you? You may respond by saying you understand how keeping the commandments (on how to treat your wife and how to treat your children) help overcome iniquity, but what has love for God got to do with it? The answer is simple. Love for God should be the reason, the primary motive, for keeping His commandments.

## 3. How your father treated his authorities

If your father disregarded speed limits when driving or displayed a lack of respect for the laws of the land in any way (which is being unequal to the rightful laws, i.e. iniquity) you too will have the propensity to do the same. Why? Because the iniquity of your father is visited upon you.

The same is true of his attitude, disposition, and behavior toward employers. We know the right attitude to employers to which we should be equal and compliant. They are outlined in the Scriptures:

*"Servants, be subject to your masters with all fear;*
*not only to the good and gentle,*
*but also to the froward."*
(1 Peter 2:18)

*"Servants, be obedient to them
that are your masters according to the flesh,
with fear and trembling,
in singleness of your heart, as unto Christ;*

*Not with eyeservice, as menpleasers;
but as the servants of Christ,
doing the will of God from the heart;*

*With good will doing service,
as to the Lord, and not to men:*

*Knowing that whatsoever good thing any man doeth,
the same shall he receive of the Lord,
whether he be bond or free."*
(Ephesians 6:5-8)

Employees, according to the above Scriptures, are required to be the following:

1. Obedient to employers (*masters according to the flesh*)

2. Fearful *(alertness)*

3. Single-minded *(concentrating, no diversions)*

4. As if you are doing your work for Christ (*as unto Christ*)

5. Without having to be watched (*not with eyeservice*)

6. Not as pleasing mere men (*as menpleasers*)

7. Mindful that you are really doing the will of God

8. Working with your heart in it

9. Kind in your work habits (*with good will*)

10. Understand that your rewards and promotions come from God

As employees, we are to do all that is listed, even if our employer is not good or gentle, but is instead warped or perverse.

It is of special interest to note that the principle of doing our work as unto the Lord and not unto our employer alone, is mentioned three times. Perhaps it is because we answer to a higher authority from whom also we receive promotions:

> *"For promotion cometh neither from the east,*
> *nor from the west, nor from the south.*
>
> *But God is the judge:*
> *he putteth down one, and setteth up another."*
> (Psalm 75:6-7)

## 4. How your father responded to church elders

This is a day when the proper balanced understanding of the authority relationships within the church are little known and practiced less. Yet proper authority is a good thing, in fact, ordained by the Lord:

> *"Obey them that have the rule over you,*
> *and submit yourselves:*
> *for they watch for your souls,*
> *as they that must give account,*
> *that they may do it with joy, and not with grief:*
> *for that is unprofitable for you."*
> (Hebrews 13:17)

Elders are set in the church by the Lord to teach, pray for the sick, and rule or oversee (administrate ministries). They watch out for us, for our souls. They will give an account to God. They are to be obeyed when instructing us within their scope of jurisdiction. It must be remembered that all proper authority has a defined and limited jurisdiction, scope, or dimension. The only absolute authority is God Himself. All human authorities representing Him have a defined authority. This balanced view of authority is crucial to Biblical functions. Straying from this idea of human authority being defined, and thus confined, leads to conduct from the silly to the catastrophic; from anarchy to domination.

Having established that authority must be balanced and defined, we nevertheless must be submissive to the proper authority of elders acting within their proper bounds. If your father did not respect or respond with obedience to church elders, this iniquity will be passed on to you.

## 5. How your father responded to God

Nothing could be of greater importance than how your father did or did not respond to God. If he believed in God but did not obey Him, this iniquity—a performance gap, not walking the talk— will be passed on to you. Without developing specific disciplines to overcome this handed-down propensity, you will tend to live the same hypocrisy as he. How dangerous is this iniquity!

## 6. How your father treated others

The Bible is a textbook on relationships. It covers the whole gamut: our relationship with God, with parents, with spouses, with children, with friends, with employers, with employees, with enemies, and with strangers. How we treat others is not optional. Wisdom instructs us, and love must compel us. If not, we will be out of proper social adjustment. We further learn from Scripture that we cannot treat others wrongfully and still be right with God. To sin against others, is in fact, to sin against God. A proper vertical relationship with God demands a proper horizontal relationship with all others in our lives.

Did your father treat the others in his life according to Scripture principles? Go ahead and do your own analysis of each of the others in your father's life, as listed above. You will then know what disciplines you need in your life to overcome passed-on iniquity.

## 7. What character flaws your father exhibited

Christlikeness is God's goal for each of us and all of us. This is termed in Scripture as being, *"conformed to the image of His Son"* (Romans 8:29), as opposed to being *"conformed to the world"* (Romans 12:2). What does it mean to be Christ-like? How can we measure our progress? If we identify and list the character qualities of Christ we will then have a basis of measurement.

If our fathers displayed juxtaposed behaviors, we will probably have to overcome those same flaws.

## How To Deal With Passed-On Iniquities

## 1. Understand the power of acknowledgement.

It is rare, if ever, that a problem is solved when it is not first identified. Read carefully the following Scriptures or you will miss important instructions:

*"Only **acknowledge thine iniquity**,*
*that thou hast transgressed against the LORD thy God,*
*and hast scattered thy ways to the strangers*
*under every green tree,*
*and ye have not obeyed my voice, saith the LORD."*
(Jeremiah 3:13)

*"We **acknowledge**, O LORD, our wickedness,*
*and **the iniquity of our fathers**:*
*for we have sinned against thee."*
(Jeremiah 14:20)

*"I **acknowledged** my sin unto thee,*
*and **mine iniquity have I not hid**. I said,*
*I will confess my transgressions unto the LORD;*
*and thou forgavest the iniquity of my sin. Selah."*
(Psalms 32:5)

The solution begins with our acknowledgement of iniquity, whether ours or that of our fathers. How many people do you know who know anything about iniquity, let alone what to do about it? But the more important question at the moment is whether you will acknowledge your iniquity, and in this case, the iniquities of your father, so that you can begin the resolution process.

## 2. God makes recompense for the iniquities of fathers.

God has a provision for iniquity. In His loving kindness He provides this to thousands. He gives it according to His counsel and observation of our ways. He does this without discrimination, that is, without respect of persons.

> *"Thou shewest lovingkindness unto thousands,*
> *and **recompensest the iniquity of the fathers***
> ***into the bosom of their children after them:***
> *the Great, the Mighty God,*
> *the LORD of hosts, is his name,*
>
> *Great in counsel, and mighty in work:*
> *for thine eyes are open upon*
> *all the ways of the sons of men*
> *to give every one **according to his ways,***
> ***and according to the fruit of his doings.***"
> (Jeremiah 32:18-19)

To whom does God recompense the iniquity of their fathers? God observes and watches all of us. The question, is for what is He watching? The answer is for those who love Him and keep His commandments; it is to those He makes an indemnification, a compensation, indeed, a reparation.

## 3. Evaluate your father and grandfathers.

The best way to learn is from instruction. If we don't, we will have to learn from the next teacher, experience. But experience can be very harsh, even cruel. To benefit from experience we should learn from both what we do right and what we do wrong; from what we do right to keep doing those right things; from what we do wrong to not keep doing those wrong things.

Further, we should learn from constructive evaluations of others. If you want to know what it's like to jump off the Empire State Building, it is best to stand at the bottom and watch someone else do the jumping and not try to experience it yourself! Those around us, including our fathers, provide ample learning possibilities if we will develop our powers of observation.

Learn from your father's true, right, and honorable behaviors and also, from his wrong behaviors. Observe your father, but not judgmentally or condemningly; that would be iniquity. But do observe your father and grandfathers. And if they have done wrong, do not follow their example. Note that this is the instruction of Scripture in Ezekiel 18:14-24:

> *"Now, lo, if he beget a son,*
> *that seeth all his father's sins which he hath done,*
> *and considereth, and doeth not such like . . ."*

Notice the instruction: a) See your father's sins; b) Consider; c) Don't do the same thing.

> *"That hath not eaten upon the mountains,*
> *neither hath lifted up his eyes*
> *to the idols of the house of Israel,*
> *hath not defiled his neighbour's wife . . ."*

Instead of being like your father: d) you have not served other gods or idols; e) you have not committed adultery.

> *"Neither hath oppressed any,*
> *hath not withholden the pledge,*
> *neither hath spoiled by violence,*
> *but hath given his bread to the hungry,*
> *and hath covered the naked with a garment . . ."*

f) You have not taken unfair advantage of others; g) You have paid your debts; h) You have not hurt others; i) You have helped the poor, the hungry, and those who needed clothes.

> *"That hath taken off his hand from the poor,*
> *that hath not received usury nor increase,*
> *hath executed my judgments,*
> *hath walked in my statutes;*
> *he **shall not die for the iniquity of his father,***
> ***he shall surely live."***

j) You have not been loan sharking; k) You have adjudicated fairly; l) You have followed the ways of the Lord. Then your father's iniquity will NOT affect you.

However, your father is in deep trouble if he did the things you refrained from and didn't do the right things you did. Look what will happen to him:

> *"As for his father, because he cruelly oppressed,*
> *spoiled his brother by violence,*
> *and did that which is not good among his people,*
> *lo, even **he shall die in his iniquity**.*
>
> *Yet say ye, **Why?***
> ***doth not the son bear the iniquity of the father?***
> *When the son hath done that which is lawful and right,*
> *and hath kept all my statutes,*
> *and hath done them, he shall surely live."*

A story is told of two brothers, the sons of a raging alcoholic. One son, in turn, became a raging alcoholic. The other son never touched a drop of it. When asked why, each responded the same way, "What do you expect when you had a father like mine?" How we respond to the iniquities of our fathers is vitally important.

When a son considers his father's iniquity, but does not follow the example, he will not bear the consequences of his father's iniquity.

*"The soul that sinneth, it shall die.*
**The son shall not bear the iniquity of the father,**
*neither shall the father bear the iniquity of the son:*
*the righteousness of the righteous shall be upon him,*
*and the wickedness of the wicked shall be upon him.*

*But if the wicked will turn*
*from all his sins that he hath committed,*
*and keep all my statutes,*
*and do that which is lawful and right,*
*he shall surely live, he shall not die.*

*All his transgressions that he hath committed,*
*they shall not be mentioned unto him:*
*in his righteousness that he hath done he shall live.*

*Have I any pleasure at all that the wicked*
*should die? saith the Lord GOD:*
*and not that he should return from his ways, and live?*

*But when the righteous*
*turneth away from his righteousness,*
*and committeth* **iniquity***,*
*and doeth according to all the abominations*
*that the wicked man doeth, shall he live?*
*All his righteousness that he hath done*
*shall not be mentioned:*
*in his trespass that he hath trespassed,*
*and in his sin that he hath sinned, in them shall he die."*
(Ezekiel 18:14-24)

It should not be unnoticed that the very next verses define precisely the meaning of iniquity. Here is a small part of it, although you have seen more details in chapter three.

*"Yet ye say, The way of the Lord is not equal.*
*Hear now, O house of Israel; Is not my way equal?*
*are not your ways unequal? (Ezekiel 18:25)*

*Yet saith the house of Israel,*
*The way of the Lord is not equal.*
*O house of Israel, are not my ways equal?*
*are not your ways unequal?*

*Therefore I will judge you, O house of Israel,*
*every one according to his ways, saith the Lord GOD.*

*Repent, and turn yourselves*
*from all your transgressions;*
*so **iniquity** shall not be your ruin."*
(Ezekiel 18:29-30)

## 4. Develop specific disciplines (keeping commandments).

Many of us cringe at the mere mention of keeping commandments. However, after we have had a genuine change of heart, as explained in the next chapter, we can unequivocally and joyfully assert that the commandments are not grievous to us. The commandments are grievous to the one whose heart is set in pleasing himself, because the commandments keep interfering with the wrong intentions of the heart. They are roadblocks to selfishness and narcissism. But when our hearts are set in the direction of pleasing God, the commandments become happy guidelines, to that upon which our hearts are already set.

*"For this is the love of God,*
*that we keep his commandments:*
*and his commandments are not grievous."*
(1 John 5:3)

We can say with David:

*"I delight to do thy will, O my God:*
*yea, thy law is within my heart."*
(Psalm 40:8)

*"But his delight is in the law of the LORD;*
*and in his law doth he meditate day and night."*
(Psalm 1:2)

*"I will delight myself in thy statutes:*
*I will not forget thy word."*
(Psalm 119:16)

*"Thy testimonies also are my*
*delight and my counsellors."*
(Psalm 119:24)

*"Make me to go in the path of thy commandments;*
*for therein do I delight."*
(Psalm 119:35)

*"And I will delight myself in thy commandments,*
*which I have loved."*
(Psalm 119:47)

Built into the commandments of the Lord are the antidotes to iniquities (not iniquity, which is the heart condition; but iniquities, which are the behavioral indications of the heart condition). For example, if one of your father's iniquities was dishonesty, not being equal to the truth, you will have to deal with that passed-on iniquity. If you develop the discipline of honesty, based on a commandment of the Lord, you will overcome that passed-on iniquity. There are a score of Scriptures which will help you develop honesty. Here are a couple:

*". . . for we trust we have a good conscience,*
*in all things willing to live honestly."*
(Hebrews 13:18)

*"Providing for honest things,*
*not only in the sight of the Lord,*
*but also in the sight of men."*
(2 Corinthians 8:21)

*"Provide things honest in the sight of all men."*
(Romans 12:17)

It is unreasonable to expect any of us to be excited about keeping the commandments of the Lord until we have had a change of heart. That is what will precipitate this enthusiasm.

# CHAPTER FIFTEEN

# Iniquity Free
# Living

*"That which I see not
teach thou me:
If I have done iniquity,
I will do no more."*
(Job 34:32)

S o what's it like? What's it like to be free of iniquity?

Life is now the way God designed it to be: the freedom to love God and others without a selfish, driving dynamic, pushing for its own agenda. In searching for a Biblical description, which I always want to do, I find the best summary in the eighth chapter of Romans and the second chapter of Galatians. Let me explain.

It requires a before and after to explain it, similar to the before and after pictures of weight-loss. Romans chapter seven describes the before. Here's a paraphrase: "I wanted to do what was right but couldn't. There was a law fighting against my mind that kept bringing me into captivity to the law of sin" (See verses 18-22). It was the selfish law of iniquity that kept me from having control.

The writer shouts out in desperation, *"O wretched man that I am! Who shall deliver me from the body of this death?"* (Romans 7:28).

I did the same thing. Haven't you? The picture here requires an understanding of an ancient practice. If one was caught in the act of murder, the officials would take the dead body of the murdered victim and tie it on the back of the guilty murderer. The murderer had to carry the dead body on his back for days and nights until it decayed and became disease-infested; it then, because of the attachment, spread to the body of the murderer. He died a terrible, painful, and slow death, eaten away by the decay and vermin. It's like us carrying this thing, this monkey on our backs, so to speak. And like the writer we call out, *"who shall deliver me from the body of this death?"*

Then comes the answer of the writer. And it's your answer and my answer: *"I thank God through the Lord Jesus Christ"* (Romans 7:25). And oh, sweet wonders, it continues. *"There is therefore now no condemnation to them which are in Christ Jesus . . . for the law of the Spirit of life in Christ Jesus hath made me free . . ."* (Romans 8:1-2).

And that's the after picture: freedom! It's freedom to love; freedom to do what's right. Freedom! No more a slave to selfish compulsions. This may sound strange to you, but it's like being dead but fully alive. I think it's the meaning of Galatians 2:20-21:

> *"I am crucified with Christ:*
> *nevertheless I live;*
> *yet not I, but Christ liveth in me:*
> *and the life which I now live in the flesh*
> *I live by the faith of the Son of God,*
> *who loved me, and gave himself for me.*
> *I do not frustrate the grace of God . . ."*

The hindrances to grace have been taken out of the way. Grace is working. The power of the resurrected Christ leads and guides and empowers. There is nothing to prove anymore. We are free. And we must keep that freedom:

*"Stand fast therefore in the liberty*
*wherewith Christ hath made us free,*
*and be not entangled again with the yoke of bondage."*
(Galatians 5:1)

We live dead to what was once like an open nerve. We have no buttons for anyone to push. We live anger-free, poised, controlled, confident, tranquil, and without over-care. We have a peace *"that passeth understanding"* (Philippians 4:7).

All decision-making has a new premise. We make principle-based decisions, in contrast with selfish benefit. We are now able to love, to choose the highest good of God and all others without personal profit as a motive. Instead of reacting, we respond. All the benefits outlined in chapter six automatically accrue to us. We *"walk in new-ness of life"* (Romans 6:4).

The abundant life that Jesus promised bursts forth. We lost our life to find it again. We were humbled that He would exalt us. We went down that we might rise up. We died that we might live. We are now the real deal, whole, healthy, authentic and established, no lon-ger *"living unto ourselves but unto Him which died for us and rose again"* (2 Corinthians 5:15).

He has now qualified us to inhabit the universe when we die or get raptured. Certainly He will not give eternal life to selfish persons. If He were to do so, we would contaminate the whole universe just like we have done on planet earth. But love like God loves, is all we have to do the rest of this life, and it is how we will function in all eternity. You are the work of His grace—what a gem and a jewel. You sparkle because you have now become a reflector of His light, His life!

Victory is easier now. The fundamental flaw of living your own way has been exterminated. The cause of all other misguidance has been replaced by the Royal Law of Love. Your life is no longer a question mark but an exclamation point. Your iniquities have been subdued. Enjoy!

*". . . God, having raised up his Son Jesus,*
*sent him to bless you,*
*in turning away every one of you*
*from his iniquities."*
(Acts 3:26)

Iniquity-free means living under Lordship. There are three *"lord-ships":* The Lordship of Jesus, The Lordship of God's Word, and the Lordship of Love. These three are synonymous. This is the new life. . . living under the management of God, His Word and Love.

God is the CEO (Chief Executive Officer) of our lives. I recently attended a meeting where Ed Kobel asked, "How many have a quiet time with the Lord every day?" Most of us raised our hands. Then he asked, "how long does that time last?" Some signified ten minutes, others twenty. Then Ed dropped the punch line on us. He said, "When you meet with a CEO the meeting isn't over until the CEO, says it's over."

When God is really the CEO and we listen for His instructions in life, everything changes. We are functionally different. We now have orders from headquarters. Ed, who is the president and chief operations officer of DeBartolo Development in Tampa, Florida, went on to illustrate what Father God had told him to do in a business situation. Nobody in the company could understand why he would be selling their four billion dollars worth of real estate assets and simply sit on the cash. Eight months later, they understood. The 2008 recession hit and those assets would have been depleted by up to sixty or seventy percent.

Being iniquity-free gets our subjective agenda out of the way and enables us to listen to God, hear our Father's voice, follow Him and see the wonders He'll do. Oh, the wonders!

# Chapter Sixteen

## Iniquity:
## The Condition
## Of Christendom

*"Who will rise up for me*
*against the evildoers?*
*or who will stand up for me*
*against the workers of iniquity?"*
(Psalm 94:16)

C *hristendom* is a word that expresses the Christian-influenced, comprehensive, worldwide, geopolitical power juxtaposed to heathenism, paganisms, and the whole gamut of religions other than Christianity. It has been assumed that Christendom is Christian. It is true that a segment of Christendom is truly Christian, but Christendom also includes a lot of "Christian-looking" influences that may not be Christian at all.

Based on his 1978 lecture at the University of Waterloo, Ontario, Malcolm Muggeridge wrote a book entitled, *The End of Christendom*. He explains that the founder of Christianity was Christ, but the founder of Christendom was the Emperor Constantine. He asserts that Christendom is based on Christianity but is constructed by men. Herein lie the contaminating elements that were mingled in with Christendom, making it much less than, and other than, *Christian*.

We now live in a society where genuine Christianity lies buried, somewhere entombed in the highly visible, but contaminated, identity of Christendom. In Christendom, the enthroned ego is accepted and even preferred and celebrated, in contradistinction to the Cross, upon which the ego—the *"old man"*—is to be crucified, that the new man may appear. The Words of Jesus about followers having to deny themselves, take up their crosses, and follow him (Matthew 16:24), are not in vogue or fashionable enough for the bulk of Christendom, because most of Christendom is not Christian.

Let's take a look at Scripture that places iniquity in a most obvious "Christian looking" context; but the context turns out NOT to be Christian at all:

> *"Many will say to me in that day, Lord, Lord,*
> *have we not prophesied in thy name?*
> *and in thy name have cast out devils?*
> *and in thy name done many wonderful works?*
>
> *And then will I profess unto them, I never knew you:*
> *depart from me, ye that work iniquity."*
> (Matthew 7:22-23)

Here is the description of the "Christian look" in this passage:
1. The confession of Jesus as Lord
2. The apparent exercise of spiritual gifts (prophecy)
3. The apparent exorcism of evil spirits
4. The appearance of many good deeds

However, Christ's adjudication is that all of these works were not truly Christian at all, but rather the working of iniquity. As such, the doers deserve removal and judgment. Their works *look* Christian, but they do not, as it is said, *pass the smell test*.

Is it possible to love the ministry without loving God? A minister can love the fact that he or she is listened to, gets to be the teacher and not the student, sways crowds, impresses with humor, or collects a following after some novel or even orthodox fashion. Here's a paradox:

*"For whosever shall save his life shall lose it:*
*and whoever will lose his life*
*for my sake shall find it."*
(Matthew 16:25)

So what makes iniquity so damning? It sounds so Christian, even having the look and the feel of being Christian. The answer is that iniquity is a serious violation of the first of the Ten Commandments:

*"Thou shalt have no other gods before me."*
(Exodus 20:3)

The greatest god-competitor is iniquity: man playing god, the enthronement of the ego in the place properly reserved only for God. The enthroned ego is the antichrist within us. Meanwhile, some of us copy things Christian, and well we should. It will be well for any person, group, or nation who imitates the life-principles taught by Jesus. Many a nation has been able to maintain civil order because of the practice of Christian principles. In those nations, the value of human life is esteemed, and the equality of womanhood is maintained. Some ego-driven persons, figure out that Jesus is right. However, they want to pick and choose from Christ's instructions. But Jesus is right about everything. Anyone who follows His wise instructions will reap the benefits in this life. For example, if a person forgives an offender as Jesus taught us to do, they will live without bitterness. How beneficial is that?

Genuine Christianity must be a wonderful thing, because so many try to copy it. Entire religious groups seek to imitate various aspects of Jesus' teachings. Individuals do it as well, but most are selective, because the enthroned ego wants to decide which parts to follow and which parts to ignore for their own personal advantage.

*"No gods before Me,"* is the issue. How can we tell if we have other gods before Him? It's actually quite simple. Do we adjust God to fit our preferences, or do we adjust our choices to align with Him? When we realize that some aspect of our life is not right according

to Scripture, do we immediately and joyfully make changes? Total surrender is essential to being a true follower of the Lord. The rest may be fans of the Lord, but not followers. Followers follow.

Imagine a young man saying to his fiancé, "I love you so much, I'm going to give up seven of my ten girlfriends." This is not going to work. Neither will it work when becoming a Christian. The enthroned ego wants to stay in charge. It has reservations. It allows all other kinds of lords, from bitterness to materialism to sensuality. True Christianity is repenting of **all** competing lordships, especially that of our exalted ego.

We have learned to fly through the air like birds. We have learned to swim through the seas like fish. But have not learned to walk on the earth like men and women. Instead, we walk around the planet playing little gods. And, we are told by Christendom preachers that God will help us do so! Thus we have Santa Clause evangelism which says, "If you come to Jesus, you will get . . ." Misguided leaders offer a listing of gifts, of every sort and description. How pathetic; not the gifts, for there are certainly tremendous benefits to being a true God-follower. But, pathetic, because these are offered to a self-centered narcissist who is set on gobbling up anything and everything that he perceives would be a contribution to his personal godhead. We are mad to believe that God would make Himself a slave of our selfishness, and allow us to become the masters, telling Him what to do.

Embedded in this massive, complex, Christian-looking conglomerate we call Christendom, is a group, a remnant (a small remaining quantity) of authentic followers of Christ. They have rejected the notion that they can simply "believe" in Jesus and be friends with the world. These understand the controversy; the contention that arises between self-rule and Christ's rulership. In Biblical terms they, *"have renounced the hidden things of dishonesty, not walking in craftiness, nor handling the word of God deceitfully; but by manifestation of the truth commending ourselves to every man's conscience in the sight of God"* (2 Corinthians 4:2).

They are the real deal. They are the salt that has not lost its savor and the light that's not put under a (religious) cover-up. They are not cosmetic Christians, but soldiers who'd rather die than betray their Lord or His ideals. They are conquerors over the world, the flesh, and the devil. They are not for sale. They cannot be bought— neither by gold, nor by the cheap tinsel trappings of the world. They are counterculture, yea, counter the Christendom culture which has compromised in the name of relevancy, and seeks to resemble the secular culture of our day in order to gain acceptance. Never had the church so much power over the world, as when it had nothing to do with the world. Believe me, Dear Reader, the day is coming when the true church, the authentic, will be deemed subversive to the culture and subversive to Christendom itself. Thus the justification for persecution of the non-compromising followers of Christ. And mark my words, that persecution will come from churchmen; those posing as Christians within Christendom, but are not really Christian at all.

The Scriptures claim that *". . . friendship with the world is enmity with God"* (James 4:4). Inclusionism, in its varying degrees, has become quite acceptable in Christendom. The industrialization of Christianity has also brought about the secularization of Christianity, which we more accurately define, not as Christianity, but as Christendom.

The remnant—the true followers of Christ—has no problem following instructions such as, *"Come out from among them, and be separate, saith the Lord, and touch not the unclean thing; and I will receive you"* (2 Corinthians 6:17). In contrast, can it not be said of the bulk of Christendom that they *"were mingled among the heathen, and learned their works. And served their idols: which were a snare unto them"* (Psalm 106:35-36)?

The prophesied falling away that was predicted in 2 Thessalonians 2:3, is happening today. It is followed by an apt description of one *"Who opposeth and exalteth himself above all that is called God . . . so that he as God sitteth in the temple of God, shewing himself that he is God"* (2 Thessalonians 2:4). While this is a prophesy describing the coming Antichrist, there is an amazing clue embedded in the text which has application to us.

First, let's understand the similarities between the antichrist and the god-players of our day.

1. The Antichrist is a god-player – they are also god-players.

2. He exalts himself above God – god-players also exalt themselves above God.

3. He opposes God's instructions – god-players live by their own opinions.

4. He is sitting in the temple of God – god-players are sitting in temples of God (their bodies, 1 Corinthians 6:19).

5. He shows that he is god – they show that they are god, not subject to any rule but their own.

Yikes! What a parallel! Both are anti-Christ. Now here is the Bible's clue to understanding. Three verses later it says that this, *"mystery of iniquity doth already work . . ."* (2 Thessalonians 2:7). There you have it. What is the Antichrist's condition? Iniquity! And what is the condition that makes us take over God's rightful place in our lives? Iniquity.

It is iniquity that is at work. So why doesn't God do something about it? He is going to, but not right now. The rest of verse seven tells us that *". . . He who now letteth will let, until he be taken out of the way."* Jesus is going to take the Antichrist out! The next Scripture says that, *". . . whom the Lord will consume with the spirit of his mouth, and shall destroy with the brightness of His coming."*

That destruction is to include those that *". . . received not the love of the truth, that they might be saved"* (verse 10). Significant now, is the reference to the people having *". . . strong delusion, that they should believe a lie. That they all might be damned who believe not the truth, but had pleasure in unrighteousness"* (verses 11-12).

Personally, I have extreme sensitivities about delusions. *A delusion is an idiosyncratic belief that is firmly maintained in spite of being contradicted by truth, by reality, by facts.* The great delusion of our day is a religious one that comes out of Christendom: that iniquity doesn't matter, that we can have a form of godliness, and that Jesus does not have to be Lord over our lives—yet we will be okay. The Scriptures say, "Wrong!" I say, "Wrong!" What do you say?

The stakes could not be higher. To know you are heading toward hell is one thing. But to be heading toward hell thinking, believing, and anticipating that you are heading toward heaven is quite another. Beloved, be not deceived.

The Visible Church is not the true Church. Consequently, western culture is facing a progressive breakdown. That consequential moral and ethical breakdown leads to a breakdown of law and order, which leads to the wide acceptance of degeneracy and corrupt behaviors, which will lead to a new-styled dark age, the unsustainability of which will lead to what Scripture calls *"the wrath to come."*

In the meantime, we ask in the inimitable style of Francis Schaeffer, "What Then Should We Now Do?"

**1. Love the truth.**

It will keep you from being deceived. Two verses after referencing the influence of iniquity, the Scriptures show the cause of deception: not loving the truth. *". . . with all deceivableness of unrighteousness in them that perish;* **because they received not the love of the truth**, *that they might be saved"* (2 Thessalonians 2:10).

## 2. Learn to loathe (not justify) your own iniquities and stay cleansed.

*"Then shall ye remember your own evil ways,*
*and your doings that were not good,*
*and shall **loathe yourselves** in your own sight*
***for your iniquities** and for your abominations.*

*Not for your sakes do I this, saith the Lord GOD,*
*be it known unto you:*
*be ashamed and confounded for your own ways...*

*Thus saith the Lord GOD;*
*In the day that I shall have*
*cleansed you from all your iniquities . . ."*
(Ezekiel 36:31-33)

## 3. Raise the standards.

Iniquity removes standards, because the right and wrong instructions and commandments of God interfere with its agenda. Iniquity wants to have its own way. Because iniquity has become the condition of Christendom, we must be careful not to allow their aberrant, self-centered standards to become ours. This can happen subtly through acculturation, conformity, and desensitization to truth.

*"When the enemy shall come in like a flood,*
*the Spirit of the LORD*
*shall lift up a standard against him."*
(Isaiah 59:19)

The answer is to do what the Holy Spirit does: raise back up and reinforce the fallen standards. It is the way of preventing the enemy from coming in. Truly, the enemy is seeking to come in *"like a flood."* The re-establishment of Biblical standards will prevent the enemy.

For example: *"I will set no wicked thing before my eyes"* (Psalm 101:3). Just spend a moment thinking of the protection and safety of such a commitment to this standard for the eyes. Now watch the next phrases in the same verse: *"I hate the work of them that turn aside; it shall not cleave to me."* Iniquity is what turns aside from this standard. We don't hate the people, but surely we must hate their work of turning us away from the right standards of God. Keeping this standard has marvelous benefits: what they are doing *"shall not cleave unto me."*

More wonderful standards follow: *"I will not know a wicked person,"* is a standard for friendships. Let us make sure we commit to a Biblical set of standards that cover every area of our lives.

### 4. Be true to the true gospel.

If we are wrong about the gospel, we are wrong about everything. Jude, in diligently writing about the *"common salvation,"* said it was needful to exhort us to contend for the faith. Here is the reason why: *"For there are certain men crept in unawares, who were before of old ordained to this condemnation, ungodly men, turning the grace of our God into lasciviousness, and denying the only Lord God, and our Lord Jesus Christ"* (Jude 1:4). Notice that the warning is not from an enemy without, but from within. They turn the true grace of God into a false concept of grace that gives the right to do wrong, and denies Jesus the right to rule our lives.

### 5. Check attitudes.

Here is a severe warning: next to not heeding the Biblical message on iniquity, the greatest danger is the misuse of this message by wielding it unlovingly. Remember that Jesus was sent to bless us *". . . in turning away every one of us from our iniquities"* (Acts 3:26). This is about blessing. The misuse of this message with a censorious, fault-finding, condemning, critical, disparaging, or deprecating attitude or disposition would itself be an iniquity of gross dimension. This message, like all messages from the God of love, must

195

be loving in manner as well as in motive; thus, you and I must give attention to speaking the truth in love.

> *"That we henceforth be no more children*
> *tossed to and fro, and carried about*
> *with every wind of doctrine,*
> *by the sleight of men, and cunning craftiness,*
> *whereby they lie in wait to deceive;*

> *But speaking the truth in love,*
> *may grow up into him in all things,*
> *which is the head, even Christ."*
> (Ephesians 4:14-15)

## 6. Love Jesus.

At the most fundamental core, genuine Christianity is about relationship; it's a most personal one—a love relationship. Many think they love Him. The fans of Jesus think they love Him. The bulk of Christendom may even admire Him somewhat. They admire the cross upon the steeple of the church but reject it as the instrument upon which they are to crucify their sins and their iniquities. But love, passionate and unrestrained toward Jesus, seems to be a rarity. I'm not speaking here of a slush, gush, and mush sentimentality; although our sentiment should be genuine and should go very deep.

Peter thought he loved the Lord. Remember? Peter was the one who said, *"Although all shall be offended, yet will not I"* (Mark 14:29). But Peter denied the Lord, not once, not twice, but three times! And, Dear Reader, I wish I could tell you that I was better than Peter, but I can't. I wish it were only three times, like Peter, but my sins and my iniquities have been many. How many times have I denied the Lord by usurping my own will over God's!

*"Peter went out and wept bitterly"* (Luke 22:62). And we have done that, haven't we? Our failures matter to us. There is a difference in us; and love is the reason. Love will always pick itself up again:

*"Love knows no limit to its endurance, no end to its trust, no fading of its hope; it can outlast anything. It is, in fact, the one thing that still stands when all else has fallen"* (1 Corinthians 13:4-7, J.B. Phillips Translation).

We must face the question asked of Peter in John 21:15: *". . . lovest thou Me?"* Three times Jesus asked the same question and Peter was put off: *"Peter was grieved because he said unto him the third time, 'Lovest thou me?'"* (John 21:17). It is really easy to say, "I love you," especially in church or when we are with the fans of Jesus. The words are easy. But are we loving in truth and loving in deed? Let us not be false professors!

Our love for Jesus is a reciprocal love: *"We love Him, because He first loved us"* (1 John 4:19). This love has evidences: *"For this is the love of God, that we keep His commandments: and His commandments are not grievous"* (1 John 5:3).

## 7. Live FOR Jesus.

Everything we do now is born out of our love for the Lord. Even when we help others we are really doing it as unto Him: *". . . whatsoever ye do, do all to the glory of God"* (1 Corinthians 10:31). Even if we give a cup of water to someone, we do it in His name (Mark 9:41).

Jesus said, *"For I was an hungred, and ye gave me meat: I was thirsty, and ye gave me drink: I was a stranger, and ye took me in: Naked, and ye clothed me: I was sick, and ye visited me: I was in prison, and ye came unto me"* (Matthew 25:35-36). The disciples went into confusion and asked, "When? We never gave you a coke or a sandwich or a blanket or paid for a hotel room. And you, Jesus—sick and in prison?"

Jesus then proclaimed a most amazing truth: although you did it *to* others, you really are doing it *for* me. Here is how He said it: *"Inasmuch as ye have done it unto one of the least of these, my brethren, ye have done it unto me"* (Matthew 25:40).

This is why true Christians are indomitable. For example, a Christian lady bakes and takes a pie to the neighbor who has company. Or we do some good deed. Usually if we don't get some expression of gratefulness back, we say, "Well if that's all the thanks I get, see if I ever do that again." Who did we do it for? Answer: ourselves. If we had done it for the Lord, then the thanks doesn't even matter to us. We are to do *everything* for the Lord. The response of others is hardly relevant. We simply please the One we love.

## 8. Live love.

Love is the anecdote for iniquity. Love is the opposite philosophy of iniquity. Iniquity is self-centered. Love considers the good of God and others. The famous love chapter, 1 Corinthians 13, affirms, *"Love rejoices not in iniquity."*

It is very relaxing to know that the rest of my life I just get to live love. It is the unselfish choosing of another's highest good, living without conflicts of interest, and giving to others without personal profit as a motive. Giving is everything from advice to care to monies. No one has anything to fear from us, unless they are afraid of love. We are sent as *"lambs among wolves"* (Luke 10:3). This may sound dangerous, but it is not. Peter explained it this way: *"And who is he that will harm you, if ye be followers of that which is good?"* (1 Peter 3:13).

Henry Drummond said that love was the greatest thing in the world. He was right. Love is the philosophy of God. God is love. Jesus is love. Love is what is produced in us by God's grace, and it is the primary evidence of the true Christian versus any other versions of Christendom. It is how we know we are like Christ. Speaking of Henry Drummond, here is a great quote from him: "To become Christ-like is the only thing in the whole world worth caring for, the thing before which every ambition of man is folly and all lower achievement vain." Let us live love!

## 9. Stay vigilant.

*"Examine yourselves, whether ye be in the faith; prove your own selves"* (2 Corinthians 13:5). This is a wise activity. I find myself in need of self-examination very frequently. Would you believe every day, and many times throughout the day, I must avert the tendency to revert back to my old ways, my old thinking, and my old motives? Old habits die hard. However, once the new life is practiced consistently, the developed new habits make it more difficult to revert back to the old habits. Let me illustrate.

I was in Dominica for several weeks. The missionary loaned me his jeep to drive, but because of British influence, they were driving on the left-hand side of the road. It took concentration to stay left when I had been driving on the right side of the road all of my life. It wasn't easy overcoming the habit, but it was necessary. I could recount incidences of near-tragedy, only averted by last split-second jerking of the steering wheel to the left. But I got the hang of it, and it became quite normal. At the end of the mission, I flew back to Toronto International Airport where my car was parked, started the engine, and (you probably guessed it) headed to the left side of the road instead of to the right. A few miles later I was back in the old comfort zone of driving on the right side of the road.

This is the struggle in Romans chapter seven between the *"old man"* and the *"new man."* There are not two people living in you. Some people think there are three people living in us. They think there is my old man, my new man and me. The Scriptures are actually using a literary device known as personification. In actuality, it is referring to the *old manner* and the *new manner*, the old habits versus the new habits. Developing righteous habits makes living the new life easy, the way it should be. After all, didn't Jesus tell us that His way was easy?

Jesus set up a specific mechanism for the activity of self-examination. We are instructed to take some bread and a cup of grape juice, called *"fruit of the vine"* in Scripture (this is non-alcoholic wine, because no alcoholic drink can ever represent the blood of Jesus). You can read the details of this process in 1 Corinthians 11:23-34. Sufficient to mention here a few points:

1. This was instituted by Jesus, not Paul.

2. The bread is a symbol of the body of Jesus, given on the cross for us.

3. The fruit of the vine is a symbol of Christ's blood, which cleanses us.

4. We are to examine ourselves in this context of the body and blood of our precious Savior, remembering His great love wherewith He has loved us. And it is in view of this solemn, frequent (perhaps daily) context that we *"let a man examine himself, and so let him eat of that bread and drink of that cup"* (1 Corinthians 11:28).

There is much more, of course, and each Reader should perform due diligence. For our purposes here, we concentrate on the process of self-examination. This will help us avoid both sins and iniquity. Let us examine: 1) our motives; 2) our thoughts; 3) our attitudes; 4) our words; and 5) our actions. We examine to assure love and guard against iniquity.

The deeper the searching, the better. So we pray as David prayed, *"Search me, O God, and know my heart: try me, and know my thoughts. And see if there be any wicked way in me, and lead me in the way everlasting"* (Psalm 139:23-24).

Why is vigilance so important? *"While men slept, his enemy came and sowed tares among the wheat . . ."* (Matthew 13:25). Jesus says the wheat and tares will grow together, but only until harvest. If we try to sort it out now we'll ruin the wheat as well: *"Let both grow together until harvest . . ."* (Matthew 13:30). The tares that look like the wheat are called by Jesus *"the children of the wicked one"*; the wheat, he called *"the good children of the kingdom"* (Matthew 13:38). The enemy that sowed the tares into Christendom is Satan.

No surprise there. He was the originator of iniquity. But here is what I don't want you to miss:

At the end, on judgment day, *"The Son of Man shall send forth his angels, and they shall gather out of his kingdom all things that offend, and **them which do iniquity***. *And shall cast them into a furnace of fire . . ."* (Matthew13:41-42).

The end-time judgment of Christendom will be the separation of those that do iniquity from those who are true Christians.

**10. Don't allow anyone to despise you because of this message.**

They will try. Understanding the issues of iniquity have been obscured for decades, if not centuries. I hope that you, like me, have been solemnly awakened and alerted to the magnitude of the issue. God will not give eternal life to god-players to spend the rest of eternity exercising their unaccountable, ego-driven agendas on others.

In reading and understanding the contents of this book, you are uniquely placed and positioned, equipped and readied to join the righteous revolution. You will be delighted to witness transformations in the lives of others. Rejoice! However, there is a cost, a down-side: you will become a high-value target.

1. Satan will come against you. You will be ruining his kingdom. In his kingdom, people don't have to live *for* him. They only have to live *like* him. Not many live *for* Satan (there indeed are some). But he thinks he wins, simply by getting as many as possible to live *like* him: the iniquitous, selfish, god-playing life. One third of the angels followed him, became like him, and fell: *"The angels which kept not their first estate . . ."* (Jude 1:6). Iniquity is the issue we have to deal with: pursuing our own way. The accurate description of us is found in Isaiah 53:6: *". . . we have turned every one to his own way."*

2. All the god-players around you will resist you. Why? Because you and this message will become a threat to their god-playing.

They might have to quit and give up themselves to the Lord God Almighty: *"Then said Jesus unto his disciples, If any man will come after me, let him deny himself, and take up his cross, and follow me"* (Matthew 16:24). This stands in stark contrast to the antinomian gospels of our day. By the way, whence the revival of antinomianism? The word literally means *no rules or law* (*anti* means *no* and *nomianism* means *rules or law*). The antinomian gospel is one that says you are saved by faith alone and no subsequent obedience to moral law is necessary. This false gospel enables people to believe they can be "saved" and still be god of their own lives, doing as they wish, whether it be right or wrong. Then they have the audacity to call it "grace."

True grace has evidence. True grace teaches. The Scriptures we are about to look at state this unequivocally. But this same passage, which is about iniquity, concludes with the main issue here. Don't let anyone despise you regarding this message of grace and the resolving of iniquity:

*"For the grace of God that bringeth salvation*
*hath appeared to all men,*

***Teaching us*** *that,*
*denying ungodliness and worldly lusts,*
*we should live soberly, righteously, and godly,*
*in this present world;*

*Looking for that blessed hope,*
*and the glorious appearing of the great God*
*and our Saviour Jesus Christ;*

*Who gave himself for us,*
***that he might redeem us from all iniquity,***
*and purify unto himself a peculiar people,*
*zealous of good works.*

> *These things speak, and exhort,*
> *and rebuke with all authority.*
> *Let no man despise thee."*
> (Titus 2:11-15)

Be sure to notice the context: redemption from ALL iniquity, followed by the promise that He is purifying us and making us peculiar. There are other references to our being "*a peculiar people.*" We sometimes tease my assistant that she is double peculiar.

What's most important is the ending *"these things speak."* 1) You and I need to be speaking the things we have learned herein; 2) We are to "*exhort*" others regarding this message; 3) if necessary we are to *"rebuke with all authority;"* and 4) *"Let no man despise you"* in these matters. Pay no heed to their ridicule, their mocking, or their contempt.

Will you answer the following questions in the affirmative?

> *"Who will rise up for me*
> *against the evildoers?*
> *or who will stand up for me*
> *against the workers of iniquity?"*
> (Psalm 94:16)

# Chapter Seventeen

# The National Implications Of Iniquity

*"Woe to him that buildeth a town...*
*and stablisheth a city by iniquity!"*
(Habakkuk 2:12)

Imagine a planet where all of its residents play god. This is a preposterous preoccupation, a madness, an insanity, an unsustainable craziness. The single greatest problem in the world is iniquity: everyone acting like a god, rejecting any authority unless forced upon them by a majority of other gods or by a few stronger, dominating gods; each acting above intuitively-known moral laws; selecting on their own individual basis any standards, or lack thereof, in his or her pursuit of god-ship.

Such god-acting is rarely, if ever, a comedy. But it is nearly always a tragedy, an unfolding drama based on human suffering that invokes in the spectator an accompanying catharsis, or more perversely, a pleasure. But this is not being acted out on a make-believe stage. This is not a virtual reality. It is not imagined, delusional, fake, false, fictional, or artificial; but in truth, it is real, on the real stage of time. And so the description of *tragedy* is infinitely understated. Shakespeare described it this way in act V, scene V of *Macbeth*. After the death of his wife, Macbeth contemplates his own death. To him, it was the last act of a very bad play. But death is not a play.

To-morrow, and to-morrow, and to-morrow,
Creeps in this petty pace from day to day,
To the last syllable of recorded time;
And all our yesterdays have lighted fools
The way to dusty death. Out, out, brief candle!
Life's but a walking shadow, a poor player,
That struts and frets his hour upon the stage,
And then is heard no more. It is a tale
Told by an idiot, full of sound and fury,
Signifying nothing.

The clichéd Shakespearian expression from *As You Like It*, "All the world's a stage, and all the men and women merely players" only points out the despair and disappointment that comes at the end of an ungodly life. Perhaps it is not despair at all but rather a hope, a wishful thinking that it has all been just a play; that the play is over now and it's time to go home—to nowhere. So they wish.

In the meantime, back in reality, is not this pretending, this god-playing, a massive multiplication of devilishness? To have one devil is enough, but the multiplication thereof has left us a planet reeling in the terrors of hellishness.

Now add technological development to this god-playing, this ultimization of selfish man. Now we get a synergism of devils acting together and against one another, each getting to spread his or her personal god-acts through electronic airwaves to millions waiting for an opportunity to send back their god-act. But in the vast majority of transmissions the communications are not, in fact, God-like; they are not Jesus-like. The spread of evil is compounding and re-duplicating, creating a ratio of change of astronomical proportions.

No wonder there must be death. Can you, in your wildest imagination, contemplate the eternalization of god-playing, by players who are anything and everything but that which resembles the true God? God is the living, loving, creative, merciful, benevolent, gracious, eternal being whose greatest ambition is to share His eternity with non-destructive lovers. True lovers are those who choose the highest good of all, without personal profit or self-aggrandizement dominating their every motive, and thus, their actions. To these He will give eternal life.

Beyond this snapshot of an imagined world though, what does iniquity do to a nation? I speak here of America.

The character of a nation is merely the aggregate of the characteristics of its citizens. This is particularly true in a nation whose form of government is democratic, that is to say, chosen, decided, and elected by the people. The Founding Fathers of America did not choose a democratic form of government, but rather that of a republic. How do these differ?

Democracy is derived from a Greek word, *demos kratos* which means *the rule of the people*. There are two kinds of democracy: a direct democracy and a representative democracy, the latter being that the people choose or elect officials to rule the country on their behalf.

The term *republic* comes from the Latin, *res publica,* which means *a thing of the people*. On the surface, these two seem to have very little difference. The two terms were used interchangeably, even at the time of the United States Constitutional Convention of 1787. James Madison, in Federalist Ten, one of eighty-five essays written by Madison, Alexander Hamilton, and John Jay, asserted that the difference was that *democracy* meant *direct democracy* and *republic* meant *representative government*.

Unsatisfied with this demarcation, James Wilson, two months later and prior to the Virginia Ratifying Convention, raised the issue which was finally answered by John Marshall, the future Chief Justice of the Supreme Court. Marshall declared that the "Constitution provided for a 'well regulated democracy' where no king, or president, could undermine representative government."

A democracy, unregulated, is nothing short of mob rule. A democracy regulated by a constitution and its founding documents is designed to limit the peoples' choices, and their representatives to function strictly within the scope of said constitution. The strength and durability of America has been based upon its constitution.

But iniquity has no scruples; none whatsoever. It accepts no limits. It complies with no standards. Iniquity is lawless. Iniquity is Satan personified (remember, Lucifer started this whole rebellion against rightful authority). So the American Republic, a democracy supposedly regulated by its constitution, is at crisis. This is not merely a political crisis. It is a moral crises. It is a spiritual crisis. And the crisis only exists because of iniquity, an endeavor to have our own ways regardless of the constitution, regardless of legal and moral precedents based on the constitution, and regardless of the God upon whom we called for aid, from whom we claimed that we were "endowed with inalienable rights."

Iniquity defines freedom as the right to do wrong. For fifty-plus years, iniquity has been storming the gates of the White House, ranting in the halls of Congress, infiltrating the Supreme Court, and paying off Senators and Congressional Representatives. Iniquity rallies are hosted across the country. The chants are chilling: "We want choice! We want choice!" What they are really chanting is, "We want to kill our babies! We want to kill our babies!" Of course, iniquity masquerades the facts under the guise of human rights and the right to choose. They really mean the rights of iniquity demanding the right to do wrong. They argue for the sodomization of the nation. The voice of iniquity is yelling in every state capital, every county seat, every city council, and behind closed doors. With false sympathy, and under the guise of compassion, exaggerated appeals are made for the right to drug ourselves into ecstasy. And please keep God out of our schools; no praying, no moral instruction, no ten commandments; just tell our children how wonderful and how dignified sodomy and same sex marriage can be. And please pay for it, all of it, with your tax dollars, so we aren't discriminated against.

Then iniquity utters her final threat. Did I say, "Utters?" Wrong! Iniquity screams! It boldly and belligerently yells at every politician, "If you don't give us what we want, we won't vote for you!" And so iniquity has eroded, undermined, and treasonously sold us out to nationwide bribery. Principle-based politics has ground to a near halt. Now the politician who promises the most to what iniquity demands, wins. Corruption triumphs. Money buys the best propaganda machinery, and the best propaganda wins, because everyone is for sale. We have no conscience. We have been bought for less than thirty pieces of silver. All of us! We have chosen moral strangling and death rather than life. Iniquity is not sustainable! We vote for self-interest, and let the good of the nation and others be damned.

Victims of propaganda never know that they are victims. In the destruction of nations, propaganda is more damaging than the sword or the gun. Propaganda is indeed a WMD, a Weapon of Mass Destruction. By it, people are manipulated, products are sold, beliefs are controlled, and politicians win. In order for propaganda to work, it must reach the masses. Here is how Adolph Hitler said it: "All propaganda must be popular, and it has to accommodate itself to the comprehension of the least intelligent of those whom it seeks to reach" (from *Mein Kampf*).

In America we have propaganda machines that reach from the White House, from the Corridors of Congress, from the halls of Academia, and from what was once, the sacred chambers of the Supreme Court, all the way down to the innocents of kindergarten. Anyone who disagrees is not met with a rationale but merely dismissed as an extremist, as a religious "kook," or worse. Christlikeness is out and compromised Christianity, atheism, and Islam are in.

Want to see the financial face of iniquity? Go to www.USDebtClock. org and stare. Stare! Stare at the trillions of dollars of debt we have. A trillion is the number of seconds in 33,000 years. Now multiply the number of seconds in 33,000 years times the near 20 trillion dollars of debt. In dollars, we owe the equivalent of the number of seconds in 660,000 years. Then add up the unfunded liability debt of the United States Government and multiply that by the number of seconds in 33,000 years. From whence comes that debt? They spent designated trust fund monies collected from us on that for which it was never intended.

Then add up the consumer debt, the corporate debt, the mortgage debt, and the household debt. And all of that is part of the financial face of iniquity. And *voici*. Here we is. Add up the value of every business, every property, every home, every automobile, every everything in the United States. You could buy everything in the country for about 97 trillion dollars. We owe almost twice what we are worth as a nation. It's very ugly.

Where is there hope? For we who are truly the Lord's, the redeemed, no problem. We are really citizens of another world. Our future is bright. For us the light shines bright on the hills of tomorrow. But what about America? America must do what you and I have learned to do in the Chapters on "How To Conquer Iniquity."

Alexis Charles Henri Clerel de Tocqueville, the French political thinker and historian made famous by his four volume work, *Democracy In America* said, "America is great because America is good. If America ceases to be good, America will cease to be great."

Certainly, there is a remnant. There is still some salt that has not lost its savor, some light that has not been extinguished. But generally speaking, you be the judge. You adjudicate the condition of America. Have her people ceased to be good? If so, how can America come back? The answer, my friend, is given to us in the Scriptures. The way back for America is the same way backslidden Israel had to come. We have to go down to get up. We can only humble ourselves that the Lord might exalt us in due time. America needs God. The way back begins when America begins to loathe herself, loathe her iniquity, and returns to God. Here's the Scripture:

*"And there shall ye remember your ways,*
*and all your doings,*
*wherein ye have been defiled;*
*and ye shall lothe yourselves in your own sight*
*for all your evils that ye have committed.*

*And ye shall know that I am the LORD,*
*when I have wrought with you for my name's sake,*
*not according to your wicked ways,*
*nor according to your corrupt doings . . ."*
(Ezekiel 20:43-44)

*"Then shall ye remember your own evil ways,*
*and your doings that were not good,*
*and shall **lothe yourselves in your own sight***
***for your iniquities and for your abominations."***
(Ezekiel 36:31)

## What Makes A Nation Great

Not serried tanks with flags unfurled,
Not armored ships that gird the world,
Not hoarded wealth nor busy mills,
Not cattle on a thousand hills,
Nor sages wise, nor schools nor laws,
Not boasted deeds in Freedom's cause—
All these may be, and yet the state
In the eye of God be far from great.
That Land is great which knows the Lord,
Whose songs are guided by His Word;

Where justice rules, 'twixt man and man,
Where love controls in art and plan;
Where, breathing in His native air,
Each soul finds joy in praise and prayer—
Thus may our country, good and great,
Be God's delight –man's best estate.

*(Alexander Blackburn)*

# CHAPTER EIGHTEEN

# Fare Thee Well

*"Who is a God like unto thee,*
*that pardoneth iniquity,*
*and passeth by the transgression*
*of the remnant of his heritage?*
*he retaineth not his anger for ever,*
*because he delighteth in mercy.*

*He will turn again,*
*he will have compassion upon us;*
*he will subdue our iniquities;*
*and thou wilt cast all their sins*
*into the depths of the sea."*
(Micah 7:18-19)

Dear Fellow-Traveler On The Road To Eternal Life: I don't like saying, "So long." I don't like farewells or goodbyes. The only glimmer of light in a farewell is the hope that we will meet again. I really like God's idea of eternity: no ends, forever, together with Him and with each other. Won't that be just fine?

I sometimes chide an audience during a teaching by saying, "Finally, but not immediately." After all, the Apostle Paul said, "Finally, my brethren," and then went on and wrote forty-three more verses. But here is my final word for now.

I hope, my Dear Reader (and I do mean dear), that you have felt like a companion of mine. For in this book we have walked a lot of less-traveled paths together. We have paused at times to view some new scenery. We have sat together to ponder the meanings of our lives, our values, their significances, and our futures. We have glanced rearward to re-evaluate the past and braced ourselves at looming difficulties. There have been moments of alarm when the trail has led to bold new inclines. We've had to hunker down at times to catch our breath. We've jumped over chasms of tradition. Shoulder-to-shoulder we have gazed forward to the great possibilities that God has for us, if only we will let go; let go of ourselves. For it is in trying to save our lives, we lose them; but in losing our lives, we find them. You have shared my story. It had a sordid beginning, and then came the shocking realization that I was trying to run the race on the wrong track. It still isn't always easy. Old habits die hard. Vigilance, attentiveness to my motives, and alertness to the Spirit's soft voice: these are the keys to overcoming the ongoing fierce demands of iniquity.

Many years ago, I committed to memory this poem by Lorrie Cline. It encapsulates the story of my life. And, I hope, yours. Fare Thee Well.

> I had walked life's way with an easy tread,
> Had followed where comforts and pleasures led,
> Until one day in a quiet place,
> I met the Master face to face.
>
> With station and rank and wealth for my goal,
> My thoughts were for body but none for my soul,
> I had entered to win in life's mad race,
> When I met the Master face to face.

I had built my castles and reared them high,
Until their towers had pierced the blue of the sky,
I had sworn to rule with an iron mace,
When I met the Master face to face.
I met Him and knew Him and blushed to see,

That His eyes full of sorrow were fixed on me;
And I faltered and fell at His feet that day,
And all my castles vanished away.
Melted and vanished, and in their place,

I saw naught else but the Jesus' face.
And I cried aloud, "Oh, make me meek,
To follow the steps of Thy wounded feet."

My thought is now for the souls of men,
I lost my life to find it again,
E'er since alone in that quiet place,
I met the Master face to face.
*(Lorrie Cline)*

Post Script

I hope we can meet again, perhaps, within the pages of several other books. I hope you'll watch for them. They are as follows:

1. God's Way To Riches (The Iniquity Free Way To Wealth)

2. Why You Were Born (Includes Why The World Began)

3. Jesus' Inaugural Address (The most important speech in the history of mankind)

4. The Seven Pillars of Wisdom (*"Wisdom is the principal thing: therefore get wisdom: and with all thy getting, get understanding.* Proverbs 4:7)

5. Ultimate Feminism: The Virtuous Woman

# Appendix

Appendix One:
Acknowledgements

Appendix Two:
Further Information

Appendix Three:
The Theological Truth About
The "No Lordship" Gospel

Appendix Four:
The Seven Bible Instructions
For Husbands

Appendix Five:
Sexuality In The Book of Proverbs

Appendix Six:
The King of Tyre

Appendix Seven:
The King James Bible

Appendix Eight:
List of Scriptures Concerning Iniquity

**Appendix One: Acknowledgements**

I am so deeply grateful to the following:

My Savior and Lord for His mercy and sweet deliverance;

My wife Judith, a contemporary, real-life version of the "virtuous woman" of Proverbs 31;

My father and mother, Lloyd and Janet Johnston, whose lives and ministries have been the godliest influences I've had in life. I could not escape the example of my father's life or the prayers of my mother;

My Sister Ruth, a great girl who has never in our lifetime shown any iniquity toward me;

Our daughters, Faith-Anne Reid and Charity Anne Kwapisz, about whom I have often said, "When I grow up, I'd like to be just like them." They love the Lord and keep His commandments. Of both of them, I am so proud;

Jason, whom I love dearly as my own son and continues to be the object of my prayers;

Doctor Paul Shirley, my friend and constant reminder that I needed to overcome the iniquity of procrastination and get this book written. He also completed the first read-through after the initial edit;

Kay Miller, my associate in ministry and whose insights are without price;

Sharon Woods for coming behind me, fixing any typos and rebuilding sentences;

My past ministerial colleagues, upon whom I wished I had been an iniquity-free influence;

Bill Gothard and the Institute In Basic Life Principles, who challenged me to study the subject of iniquity and without whose influence I would have floundered far more than I have;

To those who have known me through the years of my iniquity, I especially ask your forgiveness. I am embarrassed and humbled. I, who thought I knew so much, really know so little.

## Appendix Two: Further Information

Visit: www.NothingButTheTruth.org for several hundred hours of free Bible Teaching Videos by David Johnston.

## Appendix Three: The Theological Truth About The "No Lordship Gospel"

Antinomianism, the widespread error of our day, is the idea that behavior is unrelated to faith, or that Christians are not bound by any moral law. Antinomianism radically separates justification and sanctification, making practical holiness elective. John MacArthur's book, *The Gospel According to Jesus*, is a must-read for every one.

"No-lordship teachers often claim that they are the true heirs of the Reformation. It is extremely difficult to understand how anyone at all familiar with the literature of the Reformation could ever make such a claim. The writings of Luther and Calvin are filled with material that argues explicitly against many of the same errors no-lordship theology has embraced. Nowhere in their writings do we find any support for the idea that someone who is justified can remain unsanctified. That is a topic about which the Reformers had much to say. Why not let them speak for themselves?" (John McArthur, The Gospel According To The Apostles).

## Martin Luther

"Therefore, faith is something very powerful, active, restless, effective, which at once renews a person and again regenerates him, and leads him altogether into a new manner and character of life, so that it is impossible not to do good without ceasing.

". . . not that man should become good by works, but that man should thereby prove and see the difference between false and true faith. For wherever faith is right it does good. If it does no good, it is then certainly a dream and a false idea of faith . . . as Christ says, *'By their fruits ye shall know them.'* Thus we should also learn to know faith by its fruits.

"From this you see, there is a great difference between being good, and to be known as good; or to become good and to prove and show that you are good. Faith makes good, but works prove the faith and goodness to be right.

"Where works do not follow, a man cannot know whether his faith is right; yea, he may be certain that his faith is a dream, and not right as it should be. *"Faith without works is dead"* (James 2:20). That is, as the works do not follow, it is a sure sign that there is no faith there; but only empty thought and dream, which they falsely call faith. . . . Inasmuch as works naturally follow faith, as I said, it is not necessary to command them, for it is impossible for faith not to do them without being commanded, in order that we may learn to distinguish the false from the true faith" (Martin Luther, "Justification by Faith," in Classic Sermons on Faith and Doubt, ed. Warren W. Wiersbe [Grand Rapids, Mich.: Kregel, 1985], 78-83).

## John Calvin

"If you would duly understand how inseparable faith and works are, look to Christ. . . . Where zeal for integrity and holiness is not vigor, there neither is the Spirit of Christ nor Christ Himself; and wherever

Christ is not, there is no righteousness, nay, there is no faith; for faith cannot apprehend Christ for righteousness without the Spirit of sanctification" (John C. Olin, ed., A Reformation Debate [Grand Rapids, Mich.: Baker, 1966], 68).

"I must refute the nugatory distinction of the Schoolmen as to formed and unformed faith. For they imagine that persons who have no fear of God, and no sense of piety, may believe all that is necessary to be known for salvation; as if the Holy Spirit were not the witness of our adoption by enlightening our hearts unto faith. Still, however, though the whole Scripture is against them, they dogmatically give the name of faith to a persuasion devoid of the fear of God.

"I say that nothing can be imagined more absurd than their fiction. They insist that faith is an assent with which any despiser of God may receive what is delivered by Scripture.

"One of the first elements of faith is reconciliation implied in man's drawing near to God. Did they duly ponder the saying of Paul, *'With the heart man believeth unto righteousness'* (Romans 10:10), they would cease to dream of that frigid quality. We hold and maintain, in accordance with Scripture, that the pious only have faith.

"Let those who glory in such semblances of faith know that, in this respect, they are not a whit superior to devils. . . . Meanwhile, believers are taught to examine themselves carefully and humbly, lest carnal security creep in and take the place of assurance of faith. We may add, that the reprobate never have any other than a confused sense of grace laying hold of the shadow rather than the substance" (Calvin, Institutes [Beveridge], 3:2:8-11, 1:475-79).

## Arthur W. Pink

"Saving faith consists of the complete surrender of my whole being and life to the claims of God upon me: *'But first gave their own selves to the Lord'* (1 Corinthians 8:5).

"It is the unreserved acceptance of Christ as my absolute Lord, bowing to His will and receiving His yoke. Possibly someone may object, 'Then why are Christians exhorted as they are in Romans 12:1?' We answer, 'All such exhortations are simply a calling on them to continue as they began: *"As ye have therefore received Christ Jesus the Lord, so walk ye in Him"* (Colossians. 2:6). Yes, mark it well that Christ is 'received' as Lord. Oh, how far, far below the New Testament standard is this modern way of begging sinners to receive Christ as their own personal 'Saviour.' If the reader will consult his concordance, he will find that in every passage where the two titles are found together it is always 'Lord and Savior,' and never vice versa: see Luke 1:46, 47; 2 Peter 1:11; 2:20; 3:18, 27" (Practical Christianity, 20).

"The terrible thing is that so many preachers today, under the pretense of magnifying the grace of God, have represented Christ as the Minister of sin; as One who has, through His atoning sacrifice, procured an indulgence for men to continue gratifying their fleshly and worldly lusts. Provided a man professes to believe in the virgin birth and vicarious death of Christ and claims to be resting upon Him alone for salvation, he may pass for a real Christian almost anywhere today, even though his daily life may be no different from that of the moral worldling who makes no profession at all. The Devil is chloroforming thousands into hell by this very delusion. The Lord Jesus asks, *'Why call Me, Lord, Lord, and do not the things which I say?'* (Luke 6:46); and insists, *'Not every one that saith unto Me, Lord, Lord, shall enter int the kingdom of heaven; but he that doeth the will of My Father which is in heaven'* (Matthew 7:21)" (Ibid., 24-25).

"It is the bounden duty of every Christian to have no dealings with the 'evangelistic' monstrosity of the day: to withhold all moral and financial support of the same, to attend none of their meetings, to circulate none of their tracts. Those preachers who tell sinners they may be saved without forsaking their idols, without repenting, without surrendering to the Lordship of Christ are as erroneous and dangerous as others who insist that salvation is by works and that Heaven must be earned by our own efforts" (A.W. Pink, Studies on Saving Faith, 14).

## Charles Haddock Spurgeon

"Verily I say unto you, you cannot have Christ for your Savior unless you also have him as Lord" (C.H. Spurgeon, The Metropolitan Tabernacle Pulpit, vol. 47 [reprint, Pasadena, Tex.: Pilgrim, 1986], 570).

"Holiness is always present in those who are loyal guests of the great King, for *'without holiness no man shall see the Lord.'* Too many professors pacify themselves with the idea that they possess imputed righteousness, while they are indifferent to the sanctifying work of the Spirit. They refuse to put on the garment of obedience, they reject the white linen which is the righteousness of the saints. They thus reveal their self-will, their enmity to God, and their non-submission to his Son. Such men may talk what they will about justification by faith, and salvation by grace, but they are rebels at heart, they have not on the wedding dress any more than the self-righteous, whom they so eagerly condemn. The fact is, if we wish for the blessings of grace we must in our hearts submit to the rules of grace without picking and choosing" (C.H. Spurgeon, The Metropolitan Tabernacle Pulpit, vol. 17 [London: Passmore & Alabaster, 1984], 99).

"Christ Jesus did not come in order that you might continue in sin and escape the penalty of it. Many people think that when we preach salvation, we mean salvation from going to hell. We do not mean [only] that, but we mean a great deal more; we preach salvation from sin; we say that Christ is able to save a man; and we mean by that that he is able to save him from sin and to make him holy; to make him a new man. No person has any right to say, 'I am saved,' while he continues in sin as he did before" (C.H. Spurgeon, The Metropolitan Tabernacle Pulpit, vol. 11 [reprint, Pasadena, Tex.: Pilgrim, 1979], 138).

"There are some who seem willing to accept Christ as Savior who will not receive him as Lord. They will not often state the case quite as plainly as that; but, as actions speak more plainly than words, that is what their conduct practically says. How sad it is that some talk about their faith in Christ, yet their faith is not proved by their works! Some even speak as if they understood what we mean by the covenant of grace; yet, alas! There is no good evidence of grace in their lives, but very clear proof of sin (not grace) abounding. I cannot conceive it possible for anyone truly to receive Christ as Saviour and yet not to receive him as Lord. One of the first instincts of a redeemed soul is to fall at the feet of the Saviour, and gratefully and adoringly to cry, 'Blessed Master, bought with thy precious blood, I own that I am thine—thine only, thine wholly, thine forever. Lord, what wilt thou have me to do?' A man who is really saved by grace does not need to be told that he is under solemn obligations to serve Christ; the new life within him tells him that. Instead of regarding it as a burden, he gladly surrenders himself—body, soul, and spirit, to the Lord who has redeemed him, reckoning this to be his reasonable service. Speaking for myself, I can truthfully say that the moment I knew that Christ was my Savior, I was ready to say to him:

> I am Thine, and Thine alone.
> This I gladly, fully own!
> And, in all my works and ways,
> Only now would seek Thy praise.
> Help me to confess Thy name,
> Bear with joy Thy cross and shame,
> Only seek to follow Thee,
> Though reproach my portion be.

"It is not possible for us to accept Christ as our Savior unless He also becomes our King, for a very large part of salvation consists in our being saved from sin's dominion over us, and the only way in which we can be delivered from the mastery of Satan is by becoming subject to the mastery of Christ. . . . If it were possible for sin to be forgiven, and yet for the sinner to live just as he lived before, he would not really be saved" (C.H. Spurgeon, The Metropolitan Tabernacle Pulpit, vol. 56 [reprint, Pasadena, Texas: Pilgrim, 1979], 617).

## Jonathan Edwards

"As to that question, 'Whether closing with Christ in his kingly office be of the essence of justifying faith?' I would say: That accepting Christ in his kingly office, is doubtless the proper condition of having an interest in Christ's kingly office, and so the condition of that salvation which he bestows in the execution of that office; as much as accepting the forgiveness of sins, is the proper condition of the forgiveness of sin. Christ, in his kingly office, bestows salvation; and therefore, accepting him in his kingly office, by a disposition to sell all and suffer all in duty to Christ, and giving proper respect and honor to him, is the proper condition of salvation. This is manifest by Hebrews 5:9, *'And being made perfect, he became the author of eternal salvation to all them that obey him'. . ."* (Cited in John Gerstner, The Rational Biblical Theology of Jonathan Edwards [Orlando: Ligonier, 1991], 301).

## D.L. Moody

"We do not walk in the same way as before we were converted. A man or a woman who professes Christianity and yet goes on in the same old way has not been born again" (Dwight Lyman Moody and Ira David Sankey, "Signs of the New Birth," in The Gospel Awakening [L.T. Palmer & Co., 1877], 658).

## R. A. Torrey

R.A. Torrey, first president of Moody Bible Institute, instructed students on leading people to Christ: "Show them Jesus as Lord. It is not enough to know Jesus as Saviour, we must know Him as Lord also. A good verse for this purpose is Acts 2:36: *'Therefore let all the house of Israel know assuredly, that God hath made that same Jesus, whom ye have crucified, both Lord and Christ.'*

"When the inquirer has read the verse, ask him what God hath made Jesus, and hold him to it until he replies, 'Both Lord and Christ.' Then say to him, 'Are you willing to accept Him as your Divine Lord, the one to whom you will surrender your heart, your every thought, and word, and act?'" (R.A. Torrey, How to Work for Christ [Old Tappan, N.J.: Revell, n.d.], 37-38).

**A.W. Tozer**

"Allowing the expression 'Accept Christ' to stand as an honest effort to say in short what could not be so well said any other way, let us see what we mean or should mean when we use it.

"To accept Christ is to form an attachment to the Person of our Lord Jesus altogether unique in human experience. The attachment is intellectual, volitional, and emotional. The believer is intellectually convinced that Jesus is both Lord and Christ; he has set his will to follow Him at any cost and soon his heart is enjoying the exquisite sweetness of His fellowship.

"This attachment is all-inclusive in that it joyfully accepts Christ for all that He is. There is no craven division of offices whereby we may acknowledge His Saviourhood today and withhold decision on His Lordship till tomorrow. The true believer owns Christ as his All in All without reservation. He also includes all of himself, leaving no part of his being unaffected by the revolutionary transaction.

"Further, his attachment to Christ is all-exclusive. The Lord becomes to him not one of several rival interests, but the one exclusive attraction forever. He orbits around Christ as the earth around the sun, held in thrall by the magnetism of His love, drawing all his life and light and warmth from Him. In this happy state he is given other interests, it is true, but these are all determined by his relation to his Lord.

"That we accept Christ in this all-inclusive, all-exclusive way is a divine imperative. Here faith makes its leap into God through the Person and work of Christ, but it never divides the work from the

Person. It never tries to believe on the blood apart from Christ Himself, or the cross or the "finished work." It believes on the Lord Jesus Christ, the whole Christ without modification or reservation, and thus it receives and enjoys all that He did in His work of redemption, all that He is now doing in heaven for His own, and all that He does in and through them.

"To accept Christ is to know the meaning of the words *'as he is, so are we in this world'* (1 John 4:17). We accept His friends as our friends, His enemies as our enemies, His ways as our ways, His rejection as our rejection, His cross as our cross, His life as our life, and His future as our future.

"If this is what we mean when we advise the seeker to accept Christ, we had better explain it to him. He may get into deep spiritual trouble unless we do" (A.W. Tozer, That Incredible Christian [Harrisburg, Pa; Christian Publications, 1964], 18-19).

Tozer called no-lordship teaching a "discredited doctrine" that divides Christ. He described the teaching he opposed:

"It goes like this: Christ is both Saviour and Lord. A sinner may be saved by accepting Him as Saviour without yielding to Him as Lord. The practical outworking of this doctrine is that the evangelist presents and the seeker accepts a divided Christ. . . .

"Now, it seems odd that none of these teachers ever noticed that the only true object of saving faith is none other than Christ Himself; not the "saviourhood" of Christ nor the "lordship" of Christ, but Christ Himself. God does not offer salvation to the one who will believe on one of the offices of Christ, nor is an office of Christ ever presented as an object of faith. Neither are we exhorted to believe on the atonement, nor on the cross, nor on the priesthood of the Saviour. All of these are embodied in the person of Christ, but they are never separated nor is one ever isolated from the rest. Much less are we permitted to accept one of Christ's offices and reject another. The notion that we are so permitted is a modern day heresy, I repeat, and like every heresy it has had evil consequences among Christians. No heresy is ever entertained with impunity. We pay in practical failure for our theoretical errors.

"It is altogether doubtful whether any man can be saved who comes to Christ for His help but with no intention to obey Him. Christ's saviourhood is forever united to His lordship. Look at the Scriptures: *'If thou shalt confess with thy mouth the Lord Jesus, and shalt believe in thine heart that God hath raised him from the dead, thou shalt be saved. . . . for the same Lord over all is rich unto all that call upon him. For whosoever shall call upon the name of the Lord shall be saved'* (Romans 10:9-13). There the Lord is the object of faith for salvation. And when the Philippian jailer asked the way to be saved, Paul replied, *'Believe on the Lord Jesus Christ, and thou shalt be saved'* (Acts 16:31). He did not tell him to believe on the Saviour with the thought that he could later take up the matter of His lordship and settle it at his own convenience. To Paul there could be no division of offices. Christ must be Lord or He will not be Saviour" (A.W. Tozer, The Root of the Righteous [Harrisburg, Pa.: Christian Publications, 1955], 84-86).

## Appendix Four: The Seven Bible Instructions For Husbands

There are four primary passages in the New Testament on the subject of marriage: Ephesians 5:22-33, Colossians 3:18-19, 1 Peter 3:1-12, and 1 Corinthians 7:1-17.

There are five New Testament passages which address the subject of divorce: Matthew 5:31-32, Matthew 19:3-12, Mark 10:2-12, Luke 6:18, and Romans 7:1-2.

In addition, the second chapter of Malachi addresses the treacherous motives of divorce, explains the violent act of divorce and how men try to cover up that violence, discusses the consequences of divorce on children, and finally tells how God deals with the man that initiates divorce (and it is not pretty).

God has positioned the husband to be the loving, servant leader. The success of that leadership is dependent upon the husband following (actually doing) these Seven Instructions To Husbands.

## 1. Love Your Wife.

> *"Husbands, love your wives,*
> *even as Christ also loved the church,*
> *and gave himself for it."*
> (Ephesians 5:25)

There are three types of love referred to in the Scriptures. They are differentiated by the use of different Greek words.

*Agape* love, which is best defined as choosing the highest good of another person without personal profit or benefit as a motive. This is what God is like. This is genuine love, which is to be the basis of the other two kinds of love. The thirteenth chapter of First Corinthians is entirely about this kind of love, and verses 4 through 8 give fifteen attributes (or modifiers), of agape love. These fifteen attributes serve as a checklist for anyone wishing to verify true love: whether or not they truly love and/or whether or not they are truly being loved.

Of all the Bible content that we should know, agape love is the most important. Agape love is the essence of God, the evidence of a genuine Christian, and God's ruling philosophy of the universe. It is the core and fundamental foundation of all relationships. Husbands must master agape love and make it their chief modus operandi.

*Phileo* love is friendship-love or brotherly love. Comradeship is akin to phileo.

*Eros* love is the third kind of love. This is marital, or sexual, love. One of the great errors of our culture is to mistake eros for agape love.

Marriage is to contain all three loves, however the foundation of marriage is agape love. And this is the first and primary instruction for husbands: Husband agape love your wife. Always choose the highest good for her, regardless of what is or is not returned to you. In order to prevent any misunderstanding about this, Scripture tells us to follow a model: *"even as Christ also loved the church."*

The subsequent Scriptures are really modifiers of this love, a continuation of how love is to function within a marriage. Here are the instructions:

> *"Husbands, love your wives,*
> *even as Christ also loved the church,*
> *and gave himself for it;*
> *That he might sanctify and cleanse it*
> *with the washing of water by the word . . ."*
> (Ephesians 5:25-26)

## 2. Give Yourself For Your Wife.

". . . as Christ also loved the church and gave himself for it . . ."

A husband is to be a true lover of his wife and this love first manifests itself in giving, as opposed to getting. And this giving is a giving of himself. Giving of one's self includes time and energy, attention and care. Self-sacrifice is to be the constant and ongoing disposition of the husband toward his wife.

The focus of that ongoing giving of himself to his wife is manifested in his attitude and how he speaks to her.

## 3. Sanctify And Cleanse Her With The Words You Speak To Her.

To sanctify means to set apart, to put in a special category, to treat in a distinctly different manner from all others.

> *". . . that he might sanctify and cleanse it*
> *with the washing of water by the word . . ."*

The word husband literally means keeper of the garden. The wife and children are the garden over which the husband or husbandman is the keeper. Yet the following Scriptures indicate that he is a joint recipient of his endeavors:

> *"That he might present it to himself a glorious church,*
> *not having spot, or wrinkle, or any such thing;*
> *but that it should be holy and without blemish.*
> *So ought men to love their wives as their own bodies.*
> *He that loveth his wife loveth himself."*
> (Ephesians 5:27-28)

How is a husband to talk to his wife? My father used to say, "No raising of the voice unless the house is on fire." Hear the Scriptures:

> *"There is that speaketh like the piercings of a sword:*
> *but the tongue of the wise is health."*
> (Proverbs 12:18)

> *"The tongue of the wise useth knowledge aright:*
> *but the mouth of fools poureth out foolishness."*
> (Proverbs 15:2)

> *"Death and life are in the power of the tongue:*
> *and they that love it shall eat the fruit thereof.*
> *Whoso findeth a wife findeth a good thing,*
> *and obtaineth favour of the LORD."*
> (Proverbs 18:21-22)

Every man should become familiar, not only with these Biblical instructions about the use of his tongue, but also the entire third chapter of James. Worthy of notice is James 3:1, which tells us that there is greater condemnation for a leader/husband/master in how he uses his tongue.

A man's tongue and the words he speaks to his wife should be different than how he speaks to everyone else. That is the meaning of sanctifying her: setting her apart with the use of cleansing, healing words.

## 4. Be Bitter-Free Toward Your Wife.

*"Husbands, love your wives,*
*and be not bitter against them."*
(Colossians 3:19)

God usually gives specific instructions to certain people groups in the Bible to enable them to develop special disciplines that will help them overcome inherent weaknesses. In this case the indication is that bitterness toward one's wife is a high risk for husbands. Bitterness must be eliminated. Bitterness is, according to Scripture, a "root" issue, out of which grows many and diverse negative, life-destroying attitudes and behaviors. Note the Scriptures:

*"Follow peace with all men, and holiness,*
*without which no man shall see the Lord:*
*Looking diligently lest any man fail of the grace of God;*
*lest any root of bitterness springing up trouble you,*
*and thereby many be defiled . . ."*
(Hebrews 12:14-15)

If we fail to respond to God's grace (which is the knowledge and power to joyfully do what is right), bitterness is one of the three results. We must note two observations from this passage:

1. Bitterness will *"trouble"* you. This is not an understatement. You will personally be troubled and have trouble. Trouble will be in your future, always! The trouble is social, resulting in the inability to have authentic and transparent relationships. The trouble is mental, causing one to constantly review the faults, the failings, and the sins of others. The trouble is emotional, prohibiting the ability to have sustained peace. This is a wicked condition and is described in Scripture:

*"But the wicked are like the troubled sea,*
*when it cannot rest, whose waters cast up mire and dirt.*
*There is no peace, saith my God, to the wicked."*
(Isaiah 57:20-21)

The trouble is spiritual, damaging your ability to have faith or to be positive about life. It leads to attitudes of anger, wrath, resentment, vengeance, and many other evils which in turn, produce ongoing negative symptoms that range in severity from anxiety to sleep issues, to drug and alcohol abuse, to the development of hatred and malice.

2. Many will *"be defiled."* Bitterness is contagious. The ones most damaged will be those of your own household. A bitter person models irrational and damaging responses to life situations. And since we learn from what we observe more than from what we are told, the bitterness will spread. As if that were not bad enough, the *"many"* extends far out beyond family.

## 5. Spend Maximum Time With Your Wife

> *"Likewise, ye husbands, dwell with them . . ."*
> (1 Peter 3:7)

To *dwell* means more than just reside. It means to fasten one's attention on, and to speak at length with. Two people can be in the same house, and even in the same room, and yet be very far apart. Coming home from work and crashing in one's own separated, segregated, fantasy world of escape is the enemy of dwelling. Being a husband is a man's job.

Dwelling has to do with being companions. Companionship is one of the Biblical terms to describe marriage. Let's look at Malachi 2:12-16:

*"The LORD will cut off the man that doeth this . . ."* Oh-oh! Big trouble here. Why would God *"cut off"* a man? We are about to find out why. But note that it doesn't matter if the man is an executive (master), or educated (a scholar), or a philanthropist (one who is charitable, giving to God and/or others), or whether the man cries at the altar. In fact, God does not regard his offerings. He considers this man to be a whiner.

*"The LORD will cut off the man that doeth this,*
*the master and the scholar,*
*out of the tabernacles of Jacob,*
*and him that offereth an offering unto the LORD of hosts.*
*And this have ye done again,*
*covering the altar of the LORD with tears,*
*with weeping, and with crying out,*
*insomuch that he regardeth not the offering any more,*
*or receiveth it with good will at your hand."*

So what's the problem here? The man has been dealing treacherously with his wife, instead of keeping covenant and staying as her companion.

*"Yet ye say, Wherefore?*
*Because the LORD hath been witness*
*between thee and the wife of thy youth,*
*against whom thou hast dealt treacherously:*
*yet is she thy companion, and the wife of thy covenant."*

So what all is at stake here? First we learn that a man's relationship with God is damaged if he does not follow the Biblical guidelines for marriage. Secondly, we learn that the children will be damaged. The oneness of companionship between a man and his wife—a father and the mother of the children—is the necessary ingredient that will determine whether or not those children will be godly in the future.

*"And did not he make one?*
*Yet had he the residue of the spirit.*
*And wherefore one? That he might seek a godly seed.*
*Therefore take heed to your spirit,*
*and let none deal treacherously*
*against the wife of his youth."*

So now we should get it: God hates *"putting away."* This is a term that means *divorce*. But the instruction here isn't simply about a change in legal status by receiving a bill of divorcement. The *"putting away"* is the separation from the companionship of your wife, and seeking it elsewhere from others or other activities. Make no mistake: according to God, the putting aside or the putting away of one's wife is a violent act! Even though the man tries to cover up the violence of it, it is a violent act. There is no such thing as a friendly way of being unfriendly, or a nice way of being violent.

> *"For the LORD, the God of Israel,*
> *saith that he hateth putting away:*
> *for one covereth violence with his garment,*
> *saith the LORD of hosts:*
> *therefore take heed to your spirit,*
> *that ye deal not treacherously."*

## 6. Build A Knowledge Base About Her From Which You Can Decide And Act In An Informed Manner.

> *"Likewise, ye husbands,*
> *dwell with them **according to knowledge** . . ."*
> (1 Peter 3:7)

Fools hate knowledge, preferring to act without it (Proverbs 1:22). However, knowledge enables discretion (Proverbs 1:4). Here are a few pertinent Scriptures:

> *"Wise men lay up knowledge:*
> *but the mouth of the foolish is near destruction."*
> (Proverbs 10:14)

> *"Every prudent man dealeth with knowledge:*
> *but a fool layeth open his folly."*
> (Proverbs 13:16)

> *"The heart of the prudent getteth knowledge;*
> *and the ear of the wise seeketh knowledge."*
> (Proverbs 18:15)

What knowledge should a man have about his wife so that he will be able to respond to her with understanding instead of recklessness? Here is a short list; your list should have many more categories of data. Be sure to build your own knowledge base:

| | |
|---|---|
| Her parents | How she was raised |
| Any childhood traumas | Heart breaks, hurts, disappointments |
| What it's like to be female | Having a monthly cycle |
| Motherhood | Expectations |
| Her spiritual gift | Insecurities and fears |
| Need for privacy | Goals and ambitions |

## 7. Honor Your Wife.

*"Likewise, ye husbands,*
*dwell with them according to knowledge,*
***giving honour unto the wife,***
*as unto the weaker vessel,*
*and as being heirs together of the grace of life;*
*that your prayers be not hindered."*
(1 Peter 3:7)

To honor means to demonstrate value and esteem. This is how love sees. If you were in my office right now, I would pull out a very expensive bone china tea cup and set it in front of you, along with a plastic cup. I would then ask you two questions: 1) Which of the two vessels is the weaker? You would probably give me the correct answer: the expensive bone china tea cup. If you didn't give me the right answer, I would throw the plastic cup across the room and then ask you if you really thought the bone china tea cup was strong enough to withstand the same treatment. 2) Which of the two vessels is more valuable?

Here's the point: when God says that the wife is the weaker vessel, He does not mean the lesser vessel. She is fragile, just like the expensive bone china tea cup; weaker but more valuable! That is how a husband must treat his wife. In fact, he must never get over the awe that comes from realizing that God has entrusted to him, one of his daughters.

Don't miss this! When a man *"dwells with his wife according to knowledge, giving honor unto the wife as the weaker (not the lesser) vessel,"* his prayers will NOT be hindered! And just what do you think that's worth? Have no doubt about it: if a man does not honor his wife (God's daughter), God will not pay much attention to his prayers.

> *"For no man ever yet hated his own flesh;*
> *but nourisheth and cherisheth it,*
> *even as the Lord the church:*
> *For we are members of his body,*
> *of his flesh, and of his bones.*
> *For this cause shall a man leave his father and mother,*
> *and shall be joined unto his wife,*
> *and they two shall be one flesh.*
> *This is a great mystery:*
> *but I speak concerning Christ and the church.*
> *Nevertheless let every one of you*
> *in particular so love his wife even as himself;*
> *and the wife see that she reverence her husband."*
> (Ephesians 5:29-33)

## Appendix Five: Sexuality In The Book Of Proverbs

Proverbs chapters, five, six, seven and nine teach extensively on sexual matters, covering proper marital conduct as well as immoral conduct: chapters five, six, seven, and nine. We appreciate the directness of God on these matters but also the discretion with which they are addressed. The key to understanding these passages is knowing that a husband is referred to as a "fountain" (for obvious analogical reasons), and a wife as a cistern or reservoir. The husband is to restrict his sexual conduct to *"drink waters out of thine own cistern, and running waters out of thine own well."* The husband is instructed to *"Let thy fountain be blessed: and rejoice with the wife of thy youth. Let her be as the loving hind and pleasant roe; let her breasts satisfy thee at all times; and be thou ravished always with her love. And why wilt thou, my son, be ravished with a strange woman, and embrace the bosom of a stranger?"* (Proverbs 5:15, 18-20).

## Appendix Six: The King of Tyre

All that is said of the king of Tyre in Ezekiel chapter twenty-eight must be understood as having a double reference—to the earthly king of Tyre, a man (Ithobalus II, according to Josephus), and to the supernatural king, Satan or Lucifer, who ruled Tyre through the earthly monarch. It is Satan who is mostly referred to in this prophecy (Ezekiel 28:11-19), as there are many statements that could not possibly apply to an earthly man. Both the earthly and supernatural kings are referred to and addressed in this prophecy. Statements that could refer to the human being must be understood as concerning him; and those that could not be spoken of a man must be recognized as referring to the supernatural being. Then the passage will be clearly understood.

## Appendix Seven: The King James Bible

The following is a partial quote from an article, "The Bible of King James," by Adam Nicolson in the December 2011 issue of the *National Geographic Magazine:*

"Simple in vocabulary, cosmic in scale, stately in their rhythms, deeply emotional in their impact. Most of us might think we have forgotten its words, but the King James Bible has sewn itself into the fabric of the language. If a child is ever the apple of her parents' eye or an idea seems as old as the hills, if we are at death's door or at our wits' end, if we have gone through a baptism of fire or are about to bite the dust, if it seems at times that the blind are leading the blind or we are casting pearls before swine, if you are either buttering someone up or casting the first stone, the King James Bible, whether we know it or not, is speaking through us. The haves and have-nots, heads on plates, thieves in the night, scum of the earth, best until last, sackcloth and ashes, streets paved in gold, and the skin of one's teeth: All of them have been transmitted to us by the translators who did their magnificent work 400 years ago. . . .

"This was the divided inheritance King James wanted to mend, and a new Bible would do it. Ground rules were established by 1604: no contentious notes in the margins; no language inaccessible to common people; a true and accurate text, driven by an unforgivingly exacting level of scholarship. To bring this about, the King gathered an enormous translation committee: some fifty-four scholars, divided into all shades of opinion, from Puritan to the highest of High Churchmen. six subcommittees were then each asked to translate a different section of the Bible. . . .

"This was a world in which there was no gap between politics and religion. A translation of the Bible that could be true to the original Scriptures, be accessible to the people, and embody the kingliness of God would be the most effective political tool anyone in 17th-century England could imagine. 'We desire that the Scripture may speake like it selfe,' the translators wrote in the preface to the 1611 Bible, 'that it may be understood even of the very vulgar.' The qualities that allow connection to [everyone]—a sense of truth, a penetrating intimacy, and an overarching greatness—were exactly what King James's translators had in mind.

"They went about their work in a precise and orderly way. Each member of the six subcommittees, on his own, translated an entire section of the Bible. He then brought that translation to a meeting of his subcommittee, where the different versions produced by each translator were compared and one was settled on. That version was then submitted to a general revising committee for the whole Bible, which met in Stationers' Hall in London. Here the revising scholars had the suggested versions read aloud—no text visible—while holding on their laps copies of previous translations in English and other languages. The ear and the mind were the only editorial tools. They wanted the Bible to sound right. If it didn't at first hearing, a spirited editorial discussion—extraordinarily, mostly in Latin and partly in Greek—followed. A revising committee presented a final version to two bishops, then to the Archbishop of Canterbury, and then, notionally at least, to the King. The language is full of mystery and grace, but it is also a version of loving authority, and that is the great message of this book" (Adam Nicolson, "The Bible of King James," in National Geographic Magazine [December 2011], http://ngm.nationalgeographic.com/2011/12/king-james-bible/nicolson-text).

**Appendix Eight: List of All Scriptures regarding iniquity**

It should be noted that the word iniquity/iniquities occurs 334 times in the King James Bible, 330 times in the American Standard Bible, 300 times in Young's Literal Translation of the Bible, 279 in the Amplified Bible, 25 times in the NIV Bible, 10 times in The Message Bible, and 3 times in the New Living Translation Bible.

*"But in the fourth generation they shall come hither again: for the* ***iniquity*** *of the Amorites is not yet full"* (Genesis 15:16).

*"And when the morning arose, then the angels hastened Lot, saying, Arise, take thy wife, and thy two daughters, which are here; lest thou be consumed in the* ***iniquity*** *of the city"* (Genesis 19:15).

*"And Judah said, What shall we say unto my lord? what shall we speak? or how shall we clear ourselves? God hath found out the* ***iniquity*** *of thy servants: behold, we are my lord's servants, both we, and he also with whom the cup is found"* (Genesis 44:16).

*"Thou shalt not bow down thyself to them, nor serve them: for I the LORD thy God am a jealous God, visiting the* ***iniquity*** *of the fathers upon the children unto the third and fourth generation of them that hate me" (Exodus 20:5).*

*"And it shall be upon Aaron's forehead, that Aaron may bear the **iniquity** of the holy things, which the children of Israel shall hallow in all their holy gifts; and it shall be always upon his forehead, that they may be accepted before the LORD"* (Exodus 28:38).

*"And they shall be upon Aaron, and upon his sons, when they come in unto the tabernacle of the congregation, or when they come near unto the altar to minister in the holy place; that they bear not **iniquity**, and die: it shall be a statute for ever unto him and his seed after him"* (Exodus 28:43).

*"Keeping mercy for thousands, forgiving **iniquity** and transgression and sin, and that will by no means clear the guilty; visiting the **iniquity** of the fathers upon the children, and upon the children's children, unto the third and to the fourth generation"* (Exodus 34:7).

*"And he said, If now I have found grace in thy sight, O Lord, let my Lord, I pray thee, go among us; for it is a stiffnecked people; and pardon our **iniquity** and our sin, and take us for thine inheritance"* (Exodus 34:9).

*"And if a soul sin, and hear the voice of swearing, and is a witness, whether he hath seen or known of it; if he do not utter it, then he shall bear his **iniquity**"* (Leviticus 5:1).

*"And if a soul sin, and commit any of these things which are forbidden to be done by the commandments of the LORD; though he wist it not, yet is he guilty, and shall bear his **iniquity**"* (Leviticus 5:17).

*"And if any of the flesh of the sacrifice of his peace offerings be eaten at all on the third day, it shall not be accepted, neither shall it be imputed unto him that offereth it: it shall be an abomination, and the soul that eateth of it shall bear his **iniquity**"* (Leviticus 7:18).

*"Wherefore have ye not eaten the sin offering in the holy place, seeing it is most holy, and God hath given it you to bear the **iniquity** of the congregation, to make atonement for them before the LORD?"* (Leviticus 10:17).

*"And Aaron shall lay both his hands upon the head of the live goat, and confess over him all the **iniquities** of the children of Israel, and all their transgressions in all their sins, putting them upon the head of the goat, and shall send him away by the hand of a fit man into the wilderness"* (Leviticus 16:21).

*"And the goat shall bear upon him all their **iniquities** unto a land not inhabited: and he shall let go the goat in the wilderness"* (Leviticus 16:22).

*"But if he wash them not, nor bathe his flesh; then he shall bear his **iniquity**"* (Leviticus 17:16).

*"And the land is defiled: therefore I do visit the **iniquity** thereof upon it, and the land itself vomiteth out her inhabitants"* (Leviticus 18:25).

*"Therefore every one that eateth it shall bear his **iniquity**, because he hath profaned the hallowed thing of the LORD: and that soul shall be cut off from among his people"* (Leviticus 19:8).

*"And if a man shall take his sister, his father's daughter, or his mother's daughter, and see her nakedness, and she see his nakedness; it is a wicked thing; and they shall be cut off in the sight of their people: he hath uncovered his sister's nakedness; he shall bear his **iniquity**"* (Leviticus 20:17).

*"And thou shalt not uncover the nakedness of thy mother's sister, nor of thy father's sister: for he uncovereth his near kin: they shall bear their **iniquity**"* Leviticus 20:19).

*"Or suffer them to bear the **iniquity** of trespass, when they eat their holy things: for I the LORD do sanctify them"* (Leviticus 22:16).

*"And they that are left of you shall pine away in their **iniquity** in your enemies' lands; and also in the **iniquities** of their fathers shall they pine away with them"* (Leviticus 26:39).

*"If they shall confess their **iniquity**, and the **iniquity** of their fathers, with their trespass which they trespassed against me, and that also they have walked contrary unto me"* (Leviticus 26:40).

*"And that I also have walked contrary unto them, and have brought them into the land of their enemies; if then their uncircumcised hearts be humbled, and they then accept of the punishment of their **iniquity**"* (Leviticus 26:41).

*"The land also shall be left of them, and shall enjoy her sabbaths, while she lieth desolate without them: and they shall accept of the punishment of their **iniquity**: because, even because they despised my judgments, and because their soul abhorred my statutes"* (Leviticus 26:43).

*"Then shall the man bring his wife unto the priest, and he shall bring her offering for her, the tenth part of an ephah of barley meal; he shall pour no oil upon it, nor put frankincense thereon; for it is an offering of jealousy, an offering of memorial, bringing **iniquity** to remembrance"* (Numbers 5:15).

*"Then shall the man be guiltless from **iniquity**, and this woman shall bear her **iniquity**"* (Numbers 5:31).

*"The LORD is longsuffering, and of great mercy, forgiving **iniquity** and transgression, and by no means clearing the guilty, visiting the **iniquity** of the fathers upon the children unto the third and fourth generation"* (Numbers 14:18).

*"Pardon, I beseech thee, the **iniquity** of this people according unto the greatness of thy mercy, and as thou hast forgiven this people, from Egypt even until now"* (Numbers 14:19).

*"After the number of the days in which ye searched the land, even forty days, each day for a year, shall ye bear your **iniquities**, even forty years, and ye shall know my breach of promise"* (Numbers 14:34).

*"Because he hath despised the word of the LORD, and hath bro-ken his commandment, that soul shall utterly be cut off; his **iniquity** shall be upon him"* (Numbers 15:31).

*"And the LORD said unto Aaron, Thou and thy sons and thy father's house with thee shall bear the **iniquity** of the sanctuary: and thou and thy sons with thee shall bear the **iniquity** of your priesthood"* (Numbers 18:1).

*"But the Levites shall do the service of the tabernacle of the con-gregation, and they shall bear their **iniquity**: it shall be a statute for ever throughout your generations, that among the children of Israel they have no inheritance"* (Numbers 18:23).

*"He hath not beheld **iniquity** in Jacob, neither hath he seen per-verseness in Israel: the LORD his God is with him, and the shout of a king is among them"* (Numbers 23:21).

*"But if he shall any ways make them void after that he hath heard them; then he shall bear her **iniquity**"* (Numbers 30:15).

*"Thou shalt not bow down thyself unto them, nor serve them: for I the LORD thy God am a jealous God, visiting the **iniquity** of the fa-thers upon the children unto the third and fourth generation of them that hate me"* (Deuteronomy 5:9).

*"One witness shall not rise up against a man for any **iniquity**, or for any sin, in any sin that he sinneth: at the mouth of two witnesses, or at the mouth of three witnesses, shall the matter be established"* (Deuteronomy 19:15).

*"He is the Rock, his work is perfect: for all his ways are judgment: a God of truth and without **iniquity**, just and right is he"* (Deuter-onomy 32:4).

*"Is the **iniquity** of Peor too little for us, from which we are not cleansed until this day, although there was a plague in the congre-gation of the LORD"* (Joshua 22:17).

*"Did not Achan the son of Zerah commit a trespass in the accursed thing, and wrath fell on all the congregation of Israel? and that man perished not alone in his **iniquity**"* (Joshua 22:20).

*"For I have told him that I will judge his house for ever for the **iniquity** which he knoweth; because his sons made themselves vile, and he restrained them not"* (1 Samuel 3:13).

*"And therefore I have sworn unto the house of Eli, that the **iniquity** of Eli's house shall not be purged with sacrifice nor offering for ever"* (1 Samuel 3:14).

*"For rebellion is as the sin of witchcraft, and stubbornness is as **iniquity** and idolatry. Because thou hast rejected the word of the LORD, he hath also rejected thee from being king"* (1 Samuel 15:23).

*"And David fled from Naioth in Ramah, and came and said before Jonathan, What have I done? what is mine **iniquity**? and what is my sin before thy father, that he seeketh my life?"* (1 Samuel 20:1).

*"Therefore thou shalt deal kindly with thy servant; for thou hast brought thy servant into a covenant of the LORD with thee: notwithstanding, if there be in me **iniquity**, slay me thyself; for why shouldest thou bring me to thy father?"* (1 Samuel 20:8).

*"And fell at his feet, and said, Upon me, my lord, upon me let this **iniquity** be: and let thine handmaid, I pray thee, speak in thine audience, and hear the words of thine handmaid"* (1 Samuel 25:24).

*"I will be his father, and he shall be my son. If he commit **iniquity**, I will chasten him with the rod of men, and with the stripes of the children of men"* (2 Samuel 7:14).

*"And the woman of Tekoah said unto the king, My lord, O king, the **iniquity** be on me, and on my father's house: and the king and his throne be guiltless"* (2 Samuel 14:9).

*"And Absalom answered Joab, Behold, I sent unto thee, saying, Come hither, that I may send thee to the king, to say, Wherefore am I come from Geshur? it had been good for me to have been there still: now therefore let me see the king's face; and if there be any **iniquity** in me, let him kill me"* (2 Samuel 14:32).

*"And said unto the king, Let not my lord impute **iniquity** unto me, neither do thou remember that which thy servant did perversely the day that my lord the king went out of Jerusalem, that the king should take it to his heart"* (2 Samuel 19:19).

*"I was also upright before him, and have kept myself from mine **iniquity**"* (2 Samuel 22:24).

*"And David's heart smote him after that he had numbered the people. And David said unto the LORD, I have sinned greatly in that I have done: and now, I beseech thee, O LORD, take away the **iniquity** of thy servant; for I have done very foolishly"* (2 Samuel 24:10).

*"And David said unto God, I have sinned greatly, because I have done this thing: but now, I beseech thee, do away the **iniquity** of thy servant; for I have done very foolishly"* (1 Chronicles 21:8).

*"Wherefore now let the fear of the LORD be upon you; take heed and do it: for there is no **iniquity** with the LORD our God, nor respect of persons, nor taking of gifts"* (2 Chronicles 19:7).

*"And said, O my God, I am ashamed and blush to lift up my face to thee, my God: for our **iniquities** are increased over our head, and our trespass is grown up unto the heavens"* (Ezra 9:6).

*"Since the days of our fathers have we been in a great trespass unto this day; and for our **iniquities** have we, our kings, and our priests, been delivered into the hand of the kings of the lands, to the sword, to captivity, and to a spoil, and to confusion of face, as it is this day"* (Ezra 9:7).

*"And after all that is come upon us for our evil deeds, and for our great trespass, seeing that thou our God hast punished us less than our **iniquities** deserve, and hast given us such deliverance as this"* (Ezra 9:13).

*"And cover not their **iniquity**, and let not their sin be blotted out from before thee: for they have provoked thee to anger before the builders"* (Nehemiah 4:5).

*"And the seed of Israel separated themselves from all strangers, and stood and confessed their sins, and the **iniquities** of their fathers"* (Nehemiah 9:2).

*"Even as I have seen, they that plow **iniquity**, and sow wickedness, reap the same"* (Job 4:8).

*"So the poor hath hope, and **iniquity** stoppeth her mouth"* (Job 5:16).

*"Return, I pray you, let it not be **iniquity**; yea, return again, my righteousness is in it"* (Job 6:29).

*"Is there **iniquity** in my tongue? cannot my taste discern perverse things?"* (Job 6:30).

*"And why dost thou not pardon my transgression, and take away mine **iniquity**? for now shall I sleep in the dust; and thou shalt seek me in the morning, but I shall not be"* (Job 7:21).

*"That thou enquirest after mine **iniquity**, and searchest after my sin?"* (Job 10:6).

*"If I sin, then thou markest me, and thou wilt not acquit me from mine **iniquity**"* (Job 10:14).

*"And that he would shew thee the secrets of wisdom, that they are double to that which is! Know therefore that God exacteth of thee less than thine **iniquity** deserveth"* (Job 11:6).

*"If **iniquity** be in thine hand, put it far away, and let not wickedness dwell in thy tabernacles"* (Job 11:14).

*"How many are mine **iniquities** and sins? make me to know my transgression and my sin"* (Job 13:23).

*"For thou writest bitter things against me, and makest me to possess the **iniquities** of my youth"* (Job 13:26).

*"My transgression is sealed up in a bag, and thou sewest up mine **iniquity**"* (Job 14:17).

*"For thy mouth uttereth thine **iniquity**, and thou choosest the tongue of the crafty"* (Job 15:5).

*"How much more abominable and filthy is man, which drinketh **iniquity** like water?"* (Job 15:16).

*"The heaven shall reveal his **iniquity**; and the earth shall rise up against him"* (Job 20:27).

*"God layeth up his **iniquity** for his children: he rewardeth him, and he shall know it"* (Job 21:19).

*"Is not thy wickedness great? and thine **iniquities** infinite?"* (Job 22:5).

*"If thou return to the Almighty, thou shalt be built up, thou shalt put away **iniquity** far from thy tabernacles"* (Job 22:23).

*"Is not destruction to the wicked? and a strange punishment to the workers of **iniquity**?"* (Job 31:3).

*"For this is an heinous crime; yea, it is an **iniquity** to be punished by the judges"* (Job 31:11).

*"This also were an **iniquity** to be punished by the judge: for I should have denied the God that is above"* (Job 31:28).

*"If I covered my transgressions as Adam, by hiding mine **iniquity** in my bosom"* (Job 31:33).

*"I am clean without transgression, I am innocent; neither is there* **iniquity** *in me"* (Job 33:9).

*"Which goeth in company with the workers of* **iniquity***, and walketh with wicked men"* (Job 34:8).

*"Therefore hearken unto me, ye men of understanding: far be it from God, that he should do wickedness; and from the Almighty, that he should commit* **iniquity***"* (Job 34:10).

*"There is no darkness, nor shadow of death, where the workers of* **iniquity** *may hide themselves"* (Job 34:22).

*"That which I see not teach thou me: if I have done* **iniquity***, I will do no more"* (Job 34:32).

*"He openeth also their ear to discipline, and commandeth that they return from* **iniquity***"* (Job 36:10).

*"Take heed, regard not* **iniquity***: for this hast thou chosen rather than affliction"* (Job 36:21).

*"Who hath enjoined him his way? or who can say, Thou hast wrought* **iniquity***?"* (Job 36:23).

*"The foolish shall not stand in thy sight: thou hatest all workers of* **iniquity***"* (Psalm 5:5).

*"Depart from me, all ye workers of* **iniquity***; for the LORD hath heard the voice of my weeping"* (Psalm 6:8).

*"O LORD my God, if I have done this; if there be* **iniquity** *in my hand*s" (Psalm 7:3).

*"Behold, he travaileth with* **iniquity***, and hath conceived mischief, and brought forth falsehood"* (Psalm 7:14).

*"Have all the workers of* **iniquity** *no knowledge? who eat up my people as they eat bread, and call not upon the LORD"* (Psalm 14:4).

*"I was also upright before him, and I kept myself from mine **iniquity**"* (Psalm 18:23).

*"For thy name's sake, O LORD, pardon mine **iniquity**; for it is great"* (Psalm 25:11).

*"Draw me not away with the wicked, and with the workers of **iniquity**, which speak peace to their neighbours, but mischief is in their hearts"* (Psalm 28:3).

*"For my life is spent with grief, and my years with sighing: my strength faileth because of mine **iniquity**, and my bones are consumed"* (Psalm 31:10).

*"Blessed is the man unto whom the LORD imputeth not **iniquity**, and in whose spirit there is no guile"* (Psalm 32:2).

*"I acknowledged my sin unto thee, and mine **iniquity** have I not hid. I said, I will confess my transgressions unto the LORD; and thou forgavest the **iniquity** of my sin. Selah"* (Psalm 32:5).

*"For he flattereth himself in his own eyes, until his **iniquity** be found to be hateful"* (Psalm 36:2).

*"The words of his mouth are **iniquity** and deceit: he hath left off to be wise, and to do good"* (Psalm 36:3).

*"There are the workers of **iniquity** fallen: they are cast down, and shall not be able to rise"* (Psalm 36:12).

*"Fret not thyself because of evildoers, neither be thou envious against the workers of **iniquity**"* (Psalm 37:1).

*"For mine **iniquities** are gone over mine head: as an heavy burden they are too heavy for me"* (Psalm 38:4).

*"For I will declare mine **iniquity**; I will be sorry for my sin"* (Psalm 38:18).

*"When thou with rebukes dost correct man for **iniquity**, thou makest his beauty to consume away like a moth: surely every man is vanity. Selah"* (Psalm 39:11).

*"For innumerable evils have compassed me about: mine **iniquities** have taken hold upon me, so that I am not able to look up; they are more than the hairs of mine head: therefore my heart faileth me"* (Psalm 40:12).

*"And if he come to see me, he speaketh vanity: his heart gathereth **iniquity** to itself; when he goeth abroad, he telleth it"* (Psalm 41:6).

*"Wherefore should I fear in the days of evil, when the **iniquity** of my heels shall compass me about?"* (Psalm 49:5).

*"Wash me throughly from mine **iniquity**, and cleanse me from my sin"* (Psalm 51:2).

*"Behold, I was shapen in **iniquity**; and in sin did my mother conceive me"* (Psalm 51:5).

*"Hide thy face from my sins, and blot out all mine **iniquities**"* (Psalm 51:9).

*"The fool hath said in his heart, There is no God. Corrupt are they, and have done abominable **iniquity**: there is none that doeth good"* (Psalm 53:1).

*"Have the workers of **iniquity** no knowledge? who eat up my people as they eat bread: they have not called upon God"* (Psalm 53:4).

*"Because of the voice of the enemy, because of the oppression of the wicked: for they cast **iniquity** upon me, and in wrath they hate me"* (Psalm 55:3).

*"Shall they escape by **iniquity**? in thine anger cast down the people, O God"* (Psalm 56:7).

*"Deliver me from the workers of **iniquity**, and save me from bloody men"* (Psalm 59:2).

*"Hide me from the secret counsel of the wicked; from the insurrection of the workers of **iniquity**"* (Psalm 64:2).

*"They search out **iniquities**; they accomplish a diligent search: both the inward thought of every one of them, and the heart, is deep"* (Psalm 64:6).

*"**Iniquities** prevail against me: as for our transgressions, thou shalt purge them away"* (Psalm 65:3).

*"If I regard **iniquity** in my heart, the Lord will not hear me"* (Psalm 66:18).

*"Add **iniquity** unto their **iniquity**: and let them not come into thy righteousness"* (Psalm 69:27).

*"But he, being full of compassion, forgave their **iniquity**, and destroyed them not: yea, many a time turned he his anger away, and did not stir up all his wrath"* (Psalm 78:38).

*"O remember not against us former **iniquities**: let thy tender mercies speedily prevent us: for we are brought very low"* (Psalm 79:8).

*"Thou hast forgiven the **iniquity** of thy people, thou hast covered all their sin. Selah"* (Psalm 85:2).

*"Then will I visit their transgression with the rod, and their **iniquity** with stripes"* (Psalm 89:32).

*"Thou hast set our **iniquities** before thee, our secret sins in the light of thy countenance"* (Psalm 90:8).

*"When the wicked spring as the grass, and when all the workers of **iniquity** do flourish; it is that they shall be destroyed for ever"* (Psalm 92:7).

*"For, lo, thine enemies, O LORD, for, lo, thine enemies shall perish; all the workers of **iniquity** shall be scattered"* (Psalm 92:9).

*"How long shall they utter and speak hard things? and all the workers of **iniquity** boast themselves?"* (Psalm 94:4).

*"Who will rise up for me against the evildoers? or who will stand up for me against the workers of **iniquity**?"* (Psalm 94:16).

*"Shall the throne of **iniquity** have fellowship with thee, which frameth mischief by a law?"* (Psalm 94:20).

*"And he shall bring upon them their own **iniquity**, and shall cut them off in their own wickedness; yea, the LORD our God shall cut them off"* (Psalm 94:23).

*"Who forgiveth all thine **iniquities**; who healeth all thy diseases"* (Psalm 103:3).

*"He hath not dealt with us after our sins; nor rewarded us according to our **iniquities**"* (Psalm 103:10).

*"We have sinned with our fathers, we have committed **iniquity**, we have done wickedly"* (Psalm 106:6).

*"Many times did he deliver them; but they provoked him with their counsel, and were brought low for their **iniquity**"* (Psalm 106:43).

*"Fools because of their transgression, and because of their **iniquities**, are afflicted"* (Psalm 107:17).

*"The righteous shall see it, and rejoice: and all **iniquity** shall stop her mouth"* (Psalm 107:42).

*"Let the **iniquity** of his fathers be remembered with the LORD; and let not the sin of his mother be blotted out"* (Psalm 109:14).

*"They also do no **iniquity**: they walk in his ways"* (Psalm 119:3).

*"Order my steps in thy word: and let not any **iniquity** have dominion over me"* (Psalm 119:133).

*"For the rod of the wicked shall not rest upon the lot of the righteous; lest the righteous put forth their hands unto **iniquity**"* (Psalm 125:3).

*"As for such as turn aside unto their crooked ways, the LORD shall lead them forth with the workers of **iniquity**: but peace shall be upon Israel"* (Psalm 125:5).

*"If thou, LORD, shouldest mark **iniquities**, O Lord, who shall stand"* (Psalm 130:3).

*"And he shall redeem Israel from all his **iniquities**"* (Psalm 130:8).

*"Incline not my heart to any evil thing, to practise wicked works with men that work **iniquity**: and let me not eat of their dainties"* (Psalm 141:4).

*"Keep me from the snares which they have laid for me, and the gins of the workers of **iniquity**"* (Psalm 141:9).

*"His own **iniquities** shall take the wicked himself, and he shall be holden with the cords of his sins"* (Proverbs 5:22).

*"The way of the LORD is strength to the upright: but destruction shall be to the workers of **iniquity**"* (Proverbs 10:29).

*"By mercy and truth **iniquity** is purged: and by the fear of the LORD men depart from evil"* (Proverbs 16:6).

*"An ungodly witness scorneth judgment: and the mouth of the wicked devoureth **iniquity**"* (Proverbs 19:28).

*"It is joy to the just to do judgment: but destruction shall be to the workers of **iniquity**"* (Proverbs 21:15).

*"He that soweth **iniquity** shall reap vanity: and the rod of his anger shall fail"* (Proverbs 22:8).

*"And moreover I saw under the sun the place of judgment, that wickedness was there; and the place of righteousness, that **iniquity** was there"* (Ecclesiastes 3:16).

*"Ah sinful nation, a people laden with **iniquity**, a seed of evildoers, children that are corrupters: they have forsaken the LORD, they have provoked the Holy One of Israel unto anger, they are gone away backward"* (Isaiah 1:4).

*"Bring no more vain oblations; incense is an abomination unto me; the new moons and sabbaths, the calling of assemblies, I cannot away with; it is **iniquity**, even the solemn meeting"* (Isaiah 1:13).

*"Woe unto them that draw **iniquity** with cords of vanity, and sin as it were with a cart rope"* (Isaiah 5:18).

*"And he laid it upon my mouth, and said, Lo, this hath touched thy lips; and thine **iniquity** is taken away, and thy sin purged"* (Isaiah 6:7).

*"And I will punish the world for their evil, and the wicked for their **iniquity**; and I will cause the arrogancy of the proud to cease, and will lay low the haughtiness of the terrible"* (Isaiah 13:11).

*"Prepare slaughter for his children for the **iniquity** of their fathers; that they do not rise, nor possess the land, nor fill the face of the world with cities"* (Isaiah 14:21).

*"And it was revealed in mine ears by the LORD of hosts, Surely this **iniquity** shall not be purged from you till ye die, saith the Lord GOD of hosts"* (Isaiah 22:14).

*"For, behold, the LORD cometh out of his place to punish the inhabitants of the earth for their **iniquity**: the earth also shall disclose her blood, and shall no more cover her slain"* (Isaiah 26:21).

*"By this therefore shall the **iniquity** of Jacob be purged; and this is all the fruit to take away his sin; when he maketh all the stones of the altar as chalkstones that are beaten in sunder, the groves and images shall not stand up"* (Isaiah 27:9).

*"For the terrible one is brought to nought, and the scorner is consumed, and all that watch for **iniquity** are cut off"* (Isaiah 29:20).

*"Therefore this **iniquity** shall be to you as a breach ready to fall, swelling out in a high wall, whose breaking cometh suddenly at an instant"* (Isaiah 30:13).

*"Yet he also is wise, and will bring evil, and will not call back his words: but will arise against the house of the evildoers, and against the help of them that work **iniquity**"* (Isaiah 31:2).

*"For the vile person will speak villany, and his heart will work **iniquity**, to practise hypocrisy, and to utter error against the LORD, to make empty the soul of the hungry, and he will cause the drink of the thirsty to fail"* (Isaiah 32:6).

*"And the inhabitant shall not say, I am sick: the people that dwell therein shall be forgiven their **iniquity**"* (Isaiah 33:24).

*"Speak ye comfortably to Jerusalem, and cry unto her, that her warfare is accomplished, that her **iniquity** is pardoned: for she hath received of the LORD'S hand double for all her sins"* (Isaiah 40:2).

*"Thou hast bought me no sweet cane with money, neither hast thou filled me with the fat of thy sacrifices: but thou hast made me to serve with thy sins, thou hast wearied me with thine **iniquities**"* (Isaiah 43:24).

*"Thus saith the LORD, Where is the bill of your mother's divorcement, whom I have put away? or which of my creditors is it to whom I have sold you? Behold, for your **iniquities** have ye sold yourselves, and for your transgressions is your mother put away"* (Isaiah 50:1).

*"But he was wounded for our transgressions, he was bruised for our **iniquities**: the chastisement of our peace was upon him; and with his stripes we are healed"* (Isaiah 53:5).

*"All we like sheep have gone astray; we have turned every one to his own way; and the LORD hath laid on him the **iniquity** of us all"* (Isaiah 53:6).

*"He shall see of the travail of his soul, and shall be satisfied: by his knowledge shall my righteous servant justify many; for he shall bear their iniquities"* (Isaiah 53:11).

*"For the **iniquity** of his covetousness was I wroth, and smote him: I hid me, and was wroth, and he went on frowardly in the way of his heart"* (Isaiah 57:17).

*"But your **iniquities** have separated between you and your God, and your sins have hid his face from you, that he will not hear"* (Isaiah 59:2).

*"For your hands are defiled with blood, and your fingers with **iniquity**; your lips have spoken lies, your tongue hath muttered perverseness"* (Isaiah 59:3).

*"None calleth for justice, nor any pleadeth for truth: they trust in vanity, and speak lies; they conceive mischief, and bring forth **iniquity**"* (Isaiah 59:4).

*"Their webs shall not become garments, neither shall they cover themselves with their works: their works are works of **iniquity**, and the act of violence is in their hands"* (Isaiah 59:6).

*"Their feet run to evil, and they make haste to shed innocent blood: their thoughts are thoughts of **iniquity**; wasting and destruction are in their paths"* (Isaiah 59:7).

*"For our transgressions are multiplied before thee, and our sins testify against us: for our transgressions are with us; and as for our **iniquities**, we know them"* (Isaiah 59:12).

*"But we are all as an unclean thing, and all our righteousnesses are as filthy rags; and we all do fade as a leaf; and our **iniquities**, like the wind, have taken us away"* (Isaiah 64:6).

*"And there is none that calleth upon thy name, that stirreth up himself to take hold of thee: for thou hast hid thy face from us, and hast consumed us, because of our **iniquities**"* (Isaiah 64:7).

*"Be not wroth very sore, O LORD, neither remember **iniquity** for ever: behold, see, we beseech thee, we are all thy people"* (Isaiah 64:9).

*"Your **iniquities**, and the **iniquities** of your fathers together, saith the LORD, which have burned incense upon the mountains, and blasphemed me upon the hills: therefore will I measure their former work into their bosom"* (Isaiah 65:7).

*"Thus saith the LORD, What **iniquity** have your fathers found in me, that they are gone far from me, and have walked after vanity, and are become vain?"* (Jeremiah 2:5).

*"For though thou wash thee with nitre, and take thee much soap, yet thine **iniquity** is marked before me, saith the Lord GOD"* (Jeremiah 2:22).

*"Only acknowledge thine **iniquity**, that thou hast transgressed against the LORD thy God, and hast scattered thy ways to the strangers under every green tree, and ye have not obeyed my voice, saith the LORD"* (Jeremiah 3:13).

*"Your **iniquities** have turned away these things, and your sins have withholden good things from you"* (Jeremiah 5:25).

*"And they will deceive every one his neighbour, and will not speak the truth: they have taught their tongue to speak lies, and weary themselves to commit **iniquity**"* (Jeremiah 9:5).

*"They are turned back to the **iniquities** of their forefathers, which refused to hear my words; and they went after other gods to serve them: the house of Israel and the house of Judah have broken my covenant which I made with their fathers"* (Jeremiah 11:10).

*"And if thou say in thine heart, Wherefore come these things upon me? For the greatness of thine **iniquity** are thy skirts discovered, and thy heels made bare"* (Jeremiah 13:22).

*"O LORD, though our **iniquities** testify against us, do thou it for thy name's sake: for our backslidings are many; we have sinned against thee"* (Jeremiah 14:7).

*"Thus saith the LORD unto this people, Thus have they loved to wander, they have not refrained their feet, therefore the LORD doth not accept them; he will now remember their **iniquity**, and visit their sins"* (Jeremiah 14:10).

*"We acknowledge, O LORD, our wickedness, and the **iniquity** of our fathers: for we have sinned against thee"* (Jeremiah 14:20).

*"And it shall come to pass, when thou shalt shew this people all these words, and they shall say unto thee, Wherefore hath the LORD pronounced all this great evil against us? or what is our **iniquity**? or what is our sin that we have committed against the LORD our God?"* (Jeremiah 16:10).

*"For mine eyes are upon all their ways: they are not hid from my face, neither is their **iniquity** hid from mine eyes"* (Jeremiah 16:17).

*"And first I will recompense their **iniquity** and their sin double; because they have defiled my land, they have filled mine inheritance with the carcases of their detestable and abominable things"* (Jeremiah 16:18).

*"Yet, LORD, thou knowest all their counsel against me to slay me: forgive not their **iniquity**, neither blot out their sin from thy sight, but let them be overthrown before thee; deal thus with them in the time of thine anger"* (Jeremiah 18:23).

*"And it shall come to pass, when seventy years are accomplished, that I will punish the king of Babylon, and that nation, saith the LORD, for their **iniquity**, and the land of the Chaldeans, and will make it perpetual desolations"* (Jeremiah 25:12).

*"All thy lovers have forgotten thee; they seek thee not; for I have wounded thee with the wound of an enemy, with the chastisement of a cruel one, for the multitude of thine **iniquity**; because thy sins were increased"* (Jeremiah 30:14).

*"Why criest thou for thine affliction? thy sorrow is incurable for the multitude of thine **iniquity**: because thy sins were increased, I have done these things unto thee"* (Jeremiah 30:15).

*"But every one shall die for his own **iniquity**: every man that eateth the sour grape, his teeth shall be set on edge"* (Jeremiah 31:30).

*"And they shall teach no more every man his neighbour, and every man his brother, saying, Know the LORD: for they shall all know me, from the least of them unto the greatest of them, saith the LORD: for I will forgive their **iniquity**, and I will remember their sin no more"* (Jeremiah 31:34).

*"Thou shewest lovingkindness unto thousands, and recompensest the **iniquity** of the fathers into the bosom of their children after them: the Great, the Mighty God, the LORD of hosts, is his name"* (Jeremiah 32:18).

*"And I will cleanse them from all their **iniquity**, whereby they have sinned against me; and I will pardon all their **iniquities**, whereby they have sinned, and whereby they have transgressed against me"* (Jeremiah 33:8).

*"It may be that the house of Judah will hear all the evil which I purpose to do unto them; that they may return every man from his evil way; that I may forgive their **iniquity** and their sin"* (Jeremiah 36:3).

*"And I will punish him and his seed and his servants for their **iniquity**; and I will bring upon them, and upon the inhabitants of Jerusalem, and upon the men of Judah, all the evil that I have pronounced against them; but they hearkened not"* (Jeremiah 36:31).

*"In those days, and in that time, saith the LORD, the **iniquity** of Israel shall be sought for, and there shall be none; and the sins of Judah, and they shall not be found: for I will pardon them whom I reserve"* (Jeremiah 50:20).

*"Flee out of the midst of Babylon, and deliver every man his soul: be not cut off in her **iniquity**; for this is the time of the LORD'S vengeance; he will render unto her a recompence"* (Jeremiah 51:6).

*"Thy prophets have seen vain and foolish things for thee: and they have not discovered thine **iniquity**, to turn away thy captivity; but have seen for thee false burdens and causes of banishment"* (Lamentations 2:14).

*"For the punishment of the **iniquity** of the daughter of my people is greater than the punishment of the sin of Sodom, that was overthrown as in a moment, and no hands stayed on her"* (Lamentations 4:6).

*"For the sins of her prophets, and the **iniquities** of her priests, that have shed the blood of the just in the midst of her"* (Lamentations 4:13).

*"The punishment of thine **iniquity** is accomplished, O daughter of Zion; he will no more carry thee away into captivity: he will visit thine **iniquity**, O daughter of Edom; he will discover thy sins"* (Lamentations 4:22).

*"Our fathers have sinned, and are not; and we have borne their **iniquities**"* (Lamentations 5:7).

*"When I say unto the wicked, Thou shalt surely die; and thou givest him not warning, nor speakest to warn the wicked from his wicked way, to save his life; the same wicked man shall die in his **iniquity**; but his blood will I require at thine hand"* (Ezekiel 3:18).

*"Yet if thou warn the wicked, and he turn not from his wickedness, nor from his wicked way, he shall die in his **iniquity**; but thou hast delivered thy soul"* (Ezekiel 3:19).

*"Again, When a righteous man doth turn from his righteousness, and commit **iniquity**, and I lay a stumblingblock before him, he shall die: because thou hast not given him warning, he shall die in his sin, and his righteousness which he hath done shall not be remembered; but his blood will I require at thine hand"* (Ezekiel 3:20).

*"Lie thou also upon thy left side, and lay the **iniquity** of the house of Israel upon it: according to the number of the days that thou shalt lie upon it thou shalt bear their **iniquity**"* (Ezekiel 4:4).

*"For I have laid upon thee the years of their **iniquity**, according to the number of the days, three hundred and ninety days: so shalt thou bear the **iniquity** of the house of Israel"* (Ezekiel 4:5).

*"And when thou hast accomplished them, lie again on thy right side, and thou shalt bear the **iniquity** of the house of Judah forty days: I have appointed thee each day for a year"* (Ezekiel 4:6).

*"That they may want bread and water, and be astonied one with another, and consume away for their **iniquity**"* (Ezekiel 4:17).

*"For the seller shall not return to that which is sold, although they were yet alive: for the vision is touching the whole multitude thereof, which shall not return; neither shall any strengthen himself in the **iniquity** of his life"* (Ezekiel 7:13).

*"But they that escape of them shall escape, and shall be on the mountains like doves of the valleys, all of them mourning, every one for his **iniquity**"* (Ezekiel 7:16).

*"They shall cast their silver in the streets, and their gold shall be removed: their silver and their gold shall not be able to deliver them in the day of the wrath of the LORD: they shall not satisfy their souls, neither fill their bowels: because it is the stumblingblock of their **iniquity**"* (Ezekiel 7:19).

*"Then said he unto me, The **iniquity** of the house of Israel and Judah is exceeding great, and the land is full of blood, and the city full of perverseness: for they say, The LORD hath forsaken the earth, and the LORD seeth not"* (Ezekiel 9:9).

*"Son of man, these men have set up their idols in their heart, and put the stumblingblock of their **iniquity** before their face: should I be enquired of at all by them?"* (Ezekiel 14:3).

*"Therefore speak unto them, and say unto them, Thus saith the Lord GOD; Every man of the house of Israel that setteth up his idols in his heart, and putteth the stumblingblock of his **iniquity** before his face, and cometh to the prophet; I the LORD will answer him that cometh according to the multitude of his idols"* (Ezekiel 14:4).

*"For every one of the house of Israel, or of the stranger that sojourneth in Israel, which separateth himself from me, and setteth up his idols in his heart, and putteth the stumblingblock of his **iniquity** before his face, and cometh to a prophet to enquire of him concerning me; I the LORD will answer him by myself"* (Ezekiel 14:7).

*"And they shall bear the punishment of their **iniquity**: the punishment of the prophet shall be even as the punishment of him that seeketh unto him"* (Ezekiel 14:10).

*"Behold, this was the **iniquity** of thy sister Sodom, pride, fulness of bread, and abundance of idleness was in her and in her daughters, neither did she strengthen the hand of the poor and needy"* (Ezekiel 16:49).

*"He that hath not given forth upon usury, neither hath taken any increase, that hath withdrawn his hand from **iniquity**, hath executed true judgment between man and man"* (Ezekiel 18:8).

*"That hath taken off his hand from the poor, that hath not received usury nor increase, hath executed my judgments, hath walked in my statutes; he shall not die for the **iniquity** of his father, he shall surely live"* (Ezekiel 18:17).

*"As for his father, because he cruelly oppressed, spoiled his brother by violence, and did that which is not good among his people, lo, even he shall die in his **iniquity**"* (Ezekiel 18:18).

*"Yet say ye, Why? doth not the son bear the **iniquity** of the father? When the son hath done that which is lawful and right, and hath kept all my statutes, and hath done them, he shall surely live"* (Ezekiel 18:19).

*"The soul that sinneth, it shall die. The son shall not bear the **iniquity** of the father, neither shall the father bear the **iniquity** of the son: the righteousness of the righteous shall be upon him, and the wickedness of the wicked shall be upon him"* (Ezekiel 18:20).

*"But when the righteous turneth away from his righteousness, and committeth **iniquity**, and doeth according to all the abominations that the wicked man doeth, shall he live? All his righteousness that he hath done shall not be mentioned: in his trespass that he hath trespassed, and in his sin that he hath sinned, in them shall he die"* (Ezekiel 18:24).

*"When a righteous man turneth away from his righteousness, and committeth **iniquity**, and dieth in them; for his iniquity that he hath done shall he die"* (Ezekiel 18:26).

*"Therefore I will judge you, O house of Israel, every one according to his ways, saith the Lord GOD. Repent, and turn yourselves from all your transgressions; so **iniquity** shall not be your ruin"* (Ezekiel 18:30).

*"And it shall be unto them as a false divination in their sight, to them that have sworn oaths: but he will call to remembrance the **iniquity**, that they may be taken"* (Ezekiel 21:23).

*"Therefore thus saith the Lord GOD; Because ye have made your **iniquity** to be remembered, in that your transgressions are discovered, so that in all your doings your sins do appear; because, I say, that ye are come to remembrance, ye shall be taken with the hand"* (Ezekiel 21:24).

*"And thou, profane wicked prince of Israel, whose day is come, when **iniquity** shall have an end"* (Ezekiel 21:25).

*"Whiles they see vanity unto thee, whiles they divine a lie unto thee, to bring thee upon the necks of them that are slain, of the wicked, whose day is come, when their **iniquity** shall have an end"* (Ezekiel 21:29).

*"And your tires shall be upon your heads, and your shoes upon your feet: ye shall not mourn nor weep; but ye shall pine away for your **iniquities**, and mourn one toward another"* (Ezekiel 24:23).

*"Thou wast perfect in thy ways from the day that thou wast created, till **iniquity** was found in thee"* (Ezekiel 28:15).

*"Thou hast defiled thy sanctuaries by the multitude of thine **iniquities**, by the **iniquity** of thy traffick; therefore will I bring forth a fire from the midst of thee, it shall devour thee, and I will bring thee to ashes upon the earth in the sight of all them that behold thee"* (Ezekiel 28:18).

*"And it shall be no more the confidence of the house of Israel, which bringeth their **iniquity** to remembrance, when they shall look after them: but they shall know that I am the Lord GOD"* (Ezekiel 29:16).

*"And they shall not lie with the mighty that are fallen of the uncircumcised, which are gone down to hell with their weapons of war: and they have laid their swords under their heads, but their **iniquities** shall be upon their bones, though they were the terror of the mighty in the land of the living"* (Ezekiel 32:27).

*"But if the watchman see the sword come, and blow not the trumpet, and the people be not warned; if the sword come, and take any person from among them, he is taken away in his **iniquity**; but his blood will I require at the watchman's hand"* (Ezekiel 33:6).

*"When I say unto the wicked, O wicked man, thou shalt surely die; if thou dost not speak to warn the wicked from his way, that wicked man shall die in his **iniquity**; but his blood will I require at thine hand"* (Ezekiel 33:8).

*"Nevertheless, if thou warn the wicked of his way to turn from it; if he do not turn from his way, he shall die in his **iniquity**; but thou hast delivered thy soul"* (Ezekiel 33:9).

*"When I shall say to the righteous, that he shall surely live; if he trust to his own righteousness, and commit **iniquity**, all his righteousnesses shall not be remembered; but for his **iniquity** that he hath committed, he shall die for it"* (Ezekiel 33:13).

*"If the wicked restore the pledge, give again that he had robbed, walk in the statutes of life, without committing **iniquity**; he shall surely live, he shall not die"* (Ezekiel 33:15).

*"When the righteous turneth from his righteousness, and committeth **iniquity**, he shall even die thereby"* (Ezekiel 33:18).

*"Because thou hast had a perpetual hatred, and hast shed the blood of the children of Israel by the force of the sword in the time of their calamity, in the time that their **iniquity** had an end"* (Ezekiel 35:5).

*"Then shall ye remember your own evil ways, and your doings that were not good, and shall lothe yourselves in your own sight for your **iniquities** and for your abominations"* (Ezekiel 36:31).

*"Thus saith the Lord GOD; In the day that I shall have cleansed you from all your **iniquities** I will also cause you to dwell in the cities, and the wastes shall be builded"* (Ezekiel 36:33).

*"And the heathen shall know that the house of Israel went into captivity for their **iniquity**: because they trespassed against me, therefore hid I my face from them, and gave them into the hand of their enemies: so fell they all by the sword"* (Ezekiel 39:23).

*"Thou son of man, shew the house to the house of Israel, that they may be ashamed of their **iniquities**: and let them measure the pattern"* (Ezekiel 43:10).

*"And the Levites that are gone away far from me, when Israel went astray, which went astray away from me after their idols; they shall even bear their **iniquity**"* (Ezekiel 44:10).

*"Because they ministered unto them before their idols, and caused the house of Israel to fall into iniquity; therefore have I lifted up mine hand against them, saith the Lord GOD, and they shall bear their **iniquity**"* (Ezekiel 44:12).

*"Wherefore, O king, let my counsel be acceptable unto thee, and break off thy sins by righteousness, and thine **iniquities** by shewing mercy to the poor; if it may be a lengthening of thy tranquillity"* (Daniel 4:27).

*"We have sinned, and have committed **iniquity**, and have done wickedly, and have rebelled, even by departing from thy precepts and from thy judgments"* (Daniel 9:5).

*"As it is written in the law of Moses, all this evil is come upon us: yet made we not our prayer before the LORD our God, that we might turn from our **iniquities**, and understand thy truth"* (Daniel 9:13).

*"O Lord, according to all thy righteousness, I beseech thee, let thine anger and thy fury be turned away from thy city Jerusalem, thy holy mountain: because for our sins, and for the **iniquities** of our fathers, Jerusalem and thy people are become a reproach to all that are about us"* (Daniel 9:16).

*"Seventy weeks are determined upon thy people and upon thy holy city, to finish the transgression, and to make an end of sins, and to make reconciliation for **iniquity**, and to bring in everlasting righteousness, and to seal up the vision and prophecy, and to anoint the most Holy"* (Daniel 9:24).

*"They eat up the sin of my people, and they set their heart on their **iniquity**"* (Hosea 4:8).

*"And the pride of Israel doth testify to his face: therefore shall Israel and Ephraim fall in their **iniquity**; Judah also shall fall with them"* (Hosea 5:5).

*"Gilead is a city of them that work **iniquity**, and is polluted with blood"* (Hosea 6:8).

*"When I would have healed Israel, then the **iniquity** of Ephraim was discovered, and the wickedness of Samaria: for they commit falsehood; and the thief cometh in, and the troop of robbers spoileth without"* (Hosea 7:1).

*"They sacrifice flesh for the sacrifices of mine offerings, and eat it; but the LORD accepteth them not; now will he remember their **iniquity**, and visit their sins: they shall return to Egypt"* (Hosea 8:13).

*"The days of visitation are come, the days of recompence are come; Israel shall know it: the prophet is a fool, the spiritual man is mad, for the multitude of thine **iniquity**, and the great hatred"* (Hosea 9:7).

*"They have deeply corrupted themselves, as in the days of Gibeah: therefore he will remember their **iniquity**, he will visit their sins"* (Hosea 9:9).

*"O Israel, thou hast sinned from the days of Gibeah: there they stood: the battle in Gibeah against the children of **iniquity** did not overtake them"* (Hosea 10:9).

*"Ye have plowed wickedness, ye have reaped **iniquity**; ye have eaten the fruit of lies: because thou didst trust in thy way, in the multitude of thy mighty men"* (Hosea 10:13).

*"And Ephraim said, Yet I am become rich, I have found me out substance: in all my labours they shall find none **iniquity** in me that were sin"* (Hosea 12:8).

*"Is there **iniquity** in Gilead? surely they are vanity: they sacrifice bullocks in Gilgal; yea, their altars are as heaps in the furrows of the fields"* (Hosea 12:11).

*"The **iniquity** of Ephraim is bound up; his sin is hid"* (Hosea 13:12).

*"O Israel, return unto the LORD thy God; for thou hast fallen by thine **iniquity**"* (Hosea 14:1).

*"Take with you words, and turn to the LORD: say unto him, Take away all **iniquity**, and receive us graciously: so will we render the calves of our lips"* (Hosea 14:2).

*"You only have I known of all the families of the earth: therefore I will punish you for all your **iniquities**"* (Amos 3:2).

*"Woe to them that devise **iniquity**, and work evil upon their beds! when the morning is light, they practise it, because it is in the power of their hand"* (Micah 2:1).

*"They build up Zion with blood, and Jerusalem with **iniquity**"* (Micah 3:10).

*"Who is a God like unto thee, that pardoneth **iniquity**, and passeth by the transgression of the remnant of his heritage? he retaineth not his anger for ever, because he delighteth in mercy"* (Micah 7:18).

*"He will turn again, he will have compassion upon us; he will subdue our **iniquities**; and thou wilt cast all their sins into the depths of the sea"* (Micah 7:19).

*"Why dost thou shew me **iniquity**, and cause me to behold grievance? for spoiling and violence are before me: and there are that raise up strife and contention"* (Habakkuk 1:3).

*"Thou art of purer eyes than to behold evil, and canst not look on **iniquity**: wherefore lookest thou upon them that deal treacherously, and holdest thy tongue when the wicked devoureth the man that is more righteous than he?"* (Habakkuk 1:13).

*"Woe to him that buildeth a town with blood, and stablisheth a city by **iniquity**!"* (Habakkuk 2:12).

*"The just LORD is in the midst thereof; he will not do **iniquity**: every morning doth he bring his judgment to light, he faileth not; but the unjust knoweth no shame"* (Zephaniah 3:5).

*"The remnant of Israel shall not do **iniquity**, nor speak lies; neither shall a deceitful tongue be found in their mouth: for they shall feed and lie down, and none shall make them afraid"* (Zephaniah 3:13).

*"And he answered and spake unto those that stood before him, saying, Take away the filthy garments from him. And unto him he said, Behold, I have caused thine **iniquity** to pass from thee, and I will clothe thee with change of raiment"* (Zechariah 3:4).

*"For behold the stone that I have laid before Joshua; upon one stone shall be seven eyes: behold, I will engrave the graving thereof, saith the LORD of hosts, and I will remove the **iniquity** of that land in one day"* (Zechariah 3:9).

*"The law of truth was in his mouth, and **iniquity** was not found in his lips: he walked with me in peace and equity, and did turn many away from iniquity"* (Malachi 2:6).

*"And then will I profess unto them, I never knew you: depart from me, ye that work **iniquity**"* (Matthew 7:23).

*"The Son of man shall send forth his angels, and they shall gather out of his kingdom all things that offend, and them which do **iniquity**"* (Matthew 13:41).

*"Even so ye also outwardly appear righteous unto men, but within ye are full of hypocrisy and **iniquity**"* (Matthew 23:28).

*"And because **iniquity** shall abound, the love of many shall wax cold"* (Matthew 24:12).

*"But he shall say, I tell you, I know you not whence ye are; depart from me, all ye workers of **iniquity**"* (Luke 13:27).

*"Now this man purchased a field with the reward of **iniquity**; and falling headlong, he burst asunder in the midst, and all his bowels gushed out"* (Acts 1:18).

*"Unto you first God, having raised up his Son Jesus, sent him to bless you, in turning away every one of you from his **iniquities**"* (Acts 3:26).

*"For I perceive that thou art in the gall of bitterness, and in the bond of **iniquity**"* (Acts 8:23).

*"Saying, Blessed are they whose **iniquities** are forgiven, and whose sins are covered"* (Romans 4:7).

*"I speak after the manner of men because of the infirmity of your flesh: for as ye have yielded your members servants to uncleanness and to **iniquity** unto **iniquity**; even so now yield your members servants to righteousness unto holiness"* (Romans 6:19).

*"Rejoiceth not in **iniquity**, but rejoiceth in the truth"* (1 Corinthians 13:6).

*"For the mystery of **iniquity** doth already work: only he who now letteth will let, until he be taken out of the way"* (2 Thessalonians 2:7).

*"Nevertheless the foundation of God standeth sure, having this seal, The Lord knoweth them that are his. And, Let every one that nameth the name of Christ depart from **iniquity**"* (2 Timothy 2:19).

*"Who gave himself for us, that he might redeem us from all **iniquity**, and purify unto himself a peculiar people, zealous of good works"* (Titus 2:14).

*"Thou hast loved righteousness, and hated **iniquity**; therefore God, even thy God, hath anointed thee with the oil of gladness above thy fellows"* (Hebrews 1:9).

*"For I will be merciful to their unrighteousness, and their sins and their **iniquities** will I remember no more"* (Hebrews 8:12).

"And their sins and iniquities will I remember no more" (Hebrews 10:17).

*"And the tongue is a fire, a world of **iniquity**: so is the tongue among our members, that it defileth the whole body, and setteth on fire the course of nature; and it is set on fire of hell"* (James 3:6).

*"But was rebuked for his **iniquity**: the dumb ass speaking with man's voice forbad the madness of the prophet"* (2 Peter 2:16).

*"For her sins have reached unto heaven, and God hath remembered her **iniquities"*** (Revelation 18:5).